First Lessons®

Gospel Harp

For Group or Individual Study

by
Phil Duncan

Online Audio

To access the online audio recording go to:
WWW.MELBAY.COM/31052MEB

I0808773

MEL BAY®

WWW.MELBAY.COM

Preface

To the Student:

First Lessons Gospel Harp is designed as a step-by-step guide for learning the techniques of playing hymns and gospel music on the ten-hole diatonic harmonica. This comprehensive book explores harmonica techniques through hands-on playing of each song presented in this book. The purpose of this book is to help shorten or avoid the trial-and-error method of playing the harmonica, allowing everyone to become proficient in a relatively brief period. It is recommended that a student seek out a music instructor for further help. The harmonica is a very expressive instrument and can awaken the soul to worship, not only for yourself but for others. With that said, *"Every breath should be praise unto the Lord!"* *Ephesians 5:19, 20*. Enjoy!

To the Teacher:

This book is also a guide for the harmonica teacher or in fact, any music teacher. This method presents an array of pieces that have been adapted, specifically for the ten-hole diatonic harmonica. Teaching harmonica has become very popular. Using this book as a guide will help and encourage the beginning student. Each tune demonstrates essential techniques for playing the harmonica. This book fills a need by organizing the learning process of music, step by step, to assure a minimum of errors. With this book and a music teacher, the success rate is extremely high.

Phil Duncan

Foreword

Phil Duncan has a passion – and the credentials – for teaching the harmonica, as his scores of instruction materials attest. He also loves the gospel of Jesus. So, it's no wonder that he would want to write a book like this one, designed to help those who want to learn hymns, gospel songs, and old spirituals and learn to play them proficiently and with excellence. Played well, these songs can help the player and the listener to actually "hear" and enter into the joy, hope, and love of God that the gospel proclaims. That's what good gospel music *and* good gospel harmonica are all about. So, get your harp handy and learn what Phil has to offer here....and get ready to make a joyful noise!

Buddy Greene

CONTENTS

Alphabetical Song List

Holding a Diatonic Harmonica

Hold the harmonica in the "V" of the left hand. The fingers lie along the upper part of the instrument and the thumb along the lower part. (See Below)

For stability, the right hand cups around the back of the harmonica creating a chamber for sound changes. This mellows or warms the sound being produced.

Hand Position for Wah & Vibrato

Opening and closing the right hand can create a "wah" or a vibrato. The heels of the hands should be together, acting like a hinge to open and close the chamber created by the right hand. (See Below)

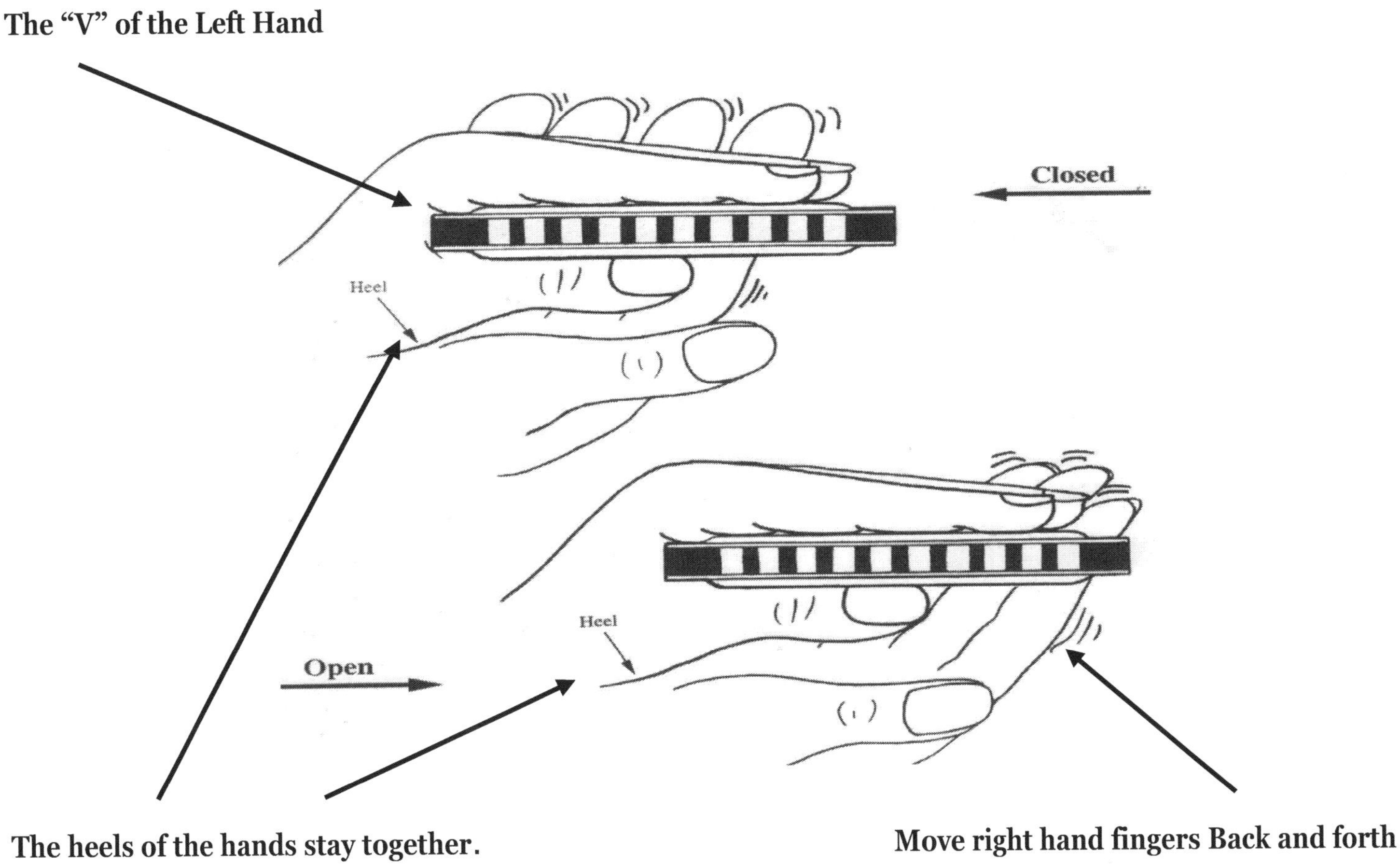

Producing a Single Tone

The harmonica is the *ONLY* instrument that is played by breathing in and out through the instrument. There are two harmonica embouchures.

Tongue Blocking

Tongue Blocking: Identify holes 2, 3, & 4 on the mouth piece of the harmonica. Put the harmonica inside your lips and bring the tongue to the harmonica. Move your tongue to the left while blowing air until hole 4 is sounding. Stop moving the tongue. Blow air in and draw air out of that single 4th hole. Keeping that position, move the harmonica to produce other single tones or holes, blow and draw, on the harmonica. Lift the tongue off the mouthpiece for the chord and then replace it to play the single tone again.
Note: Upper-case letters are blow, lower-case letters are draw.

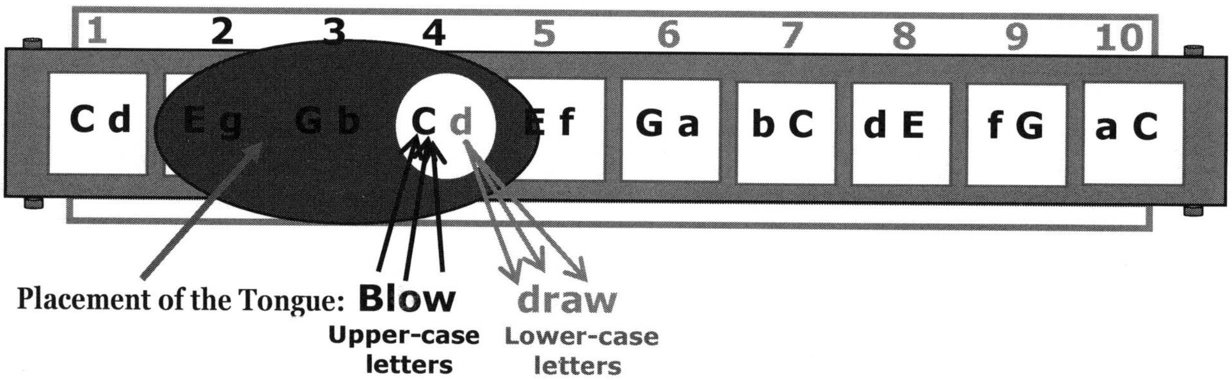

Lip Blocking

Lip Blocking: Pursing the lips can also produce a single tone. Making the opening a little taller than wider and surrounding any single hole will produce one tone, blowing or drawing. Do not let air escape around the harmonica mouth piece. ***All air*** should only go ***through*** the harmonica. Hole 4 should produce C blow and d draw notes.

The lips purse targeting around the single hole. No tongue is used.

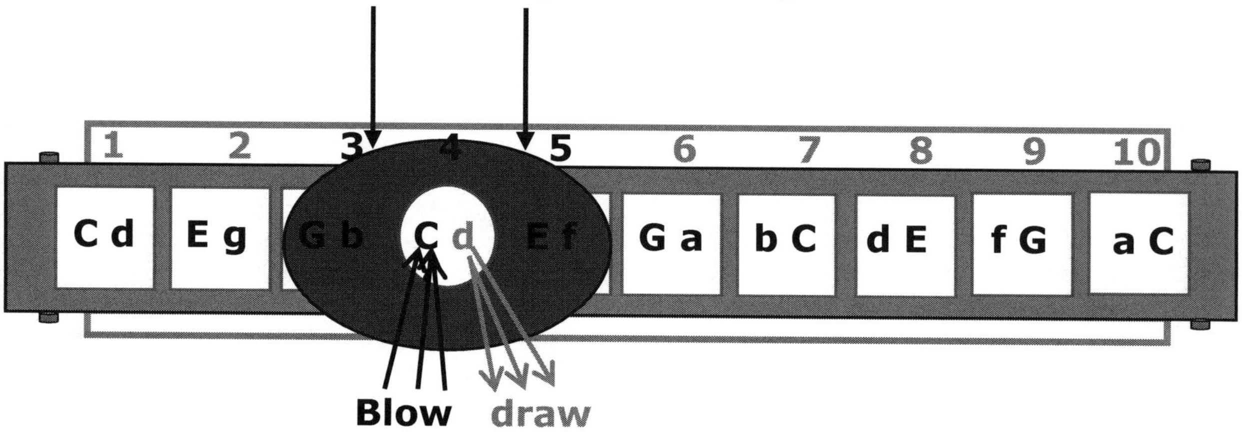

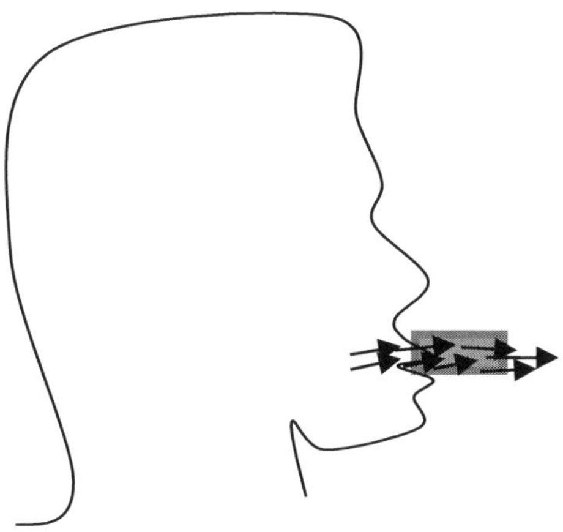

BLOWING Air (Exhale)

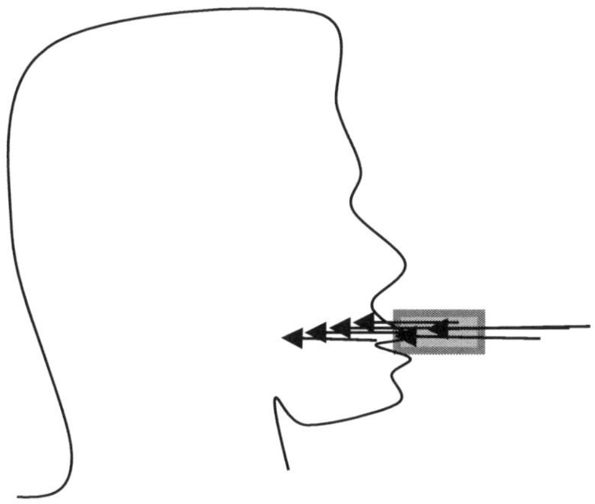

drawing air (inhale)

TABLATURE: ARROWS, NUMBERS
Blowing/Exhaling

1. Arrows pointing up indicate: ↑ Exhale/**BLOW** into the single hole

drawing/inhaling

2. Arrows pointing down mean: ↓ Inhale/**draw** air from a single hole

BASIC MUSICAL INFORMATION
Ten-Hole Harmonica

The staff uses a treble or G clef sign: 𝄞 To denote a higher sound. The lower half looks like a cursive G. This G clef sign circles the second line of the five-line staff indicating the G note. Each line/space of the staff represents a pitch or tone. The higher the line/space, the higher the pitch. There are five (5) lines and four (4) spaces. Each has a pitch name. Example: The bottom line, 1st line, is E. It is found in the 5th hole, blow on the harmonica. The bottom or first space is f, the 5th hole, draw.

The vertical lines on the horizontal staff are measure bar lines. The double bar lines *(thin & thick lines)* end the musical notation. Time Signatures and bar lines separate and indicate the beats per measure. Do not be confused when bar 3 is considered the same as measure 3. In this case, "bar" does not refer to "bar line." Two thin bar lines indicate a change such as verse to refrain. A measure is the distance between two bar lines; it measures a length of time. Measures are numbered in these tunes. Two dots on the 2nd and 3rd spaces of the staff creates a repeat sign. A whole rest indicates silence for a complete measure. A half rest sits on the third line. A quarter rest looks like a bird flying sideways and an eighth rest looks like a cursive 7.

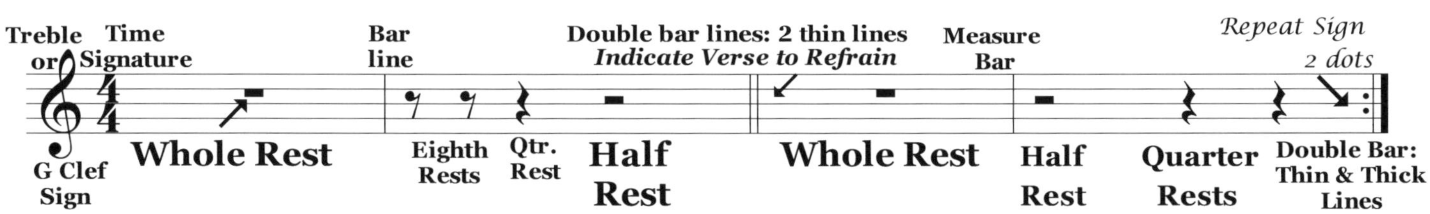

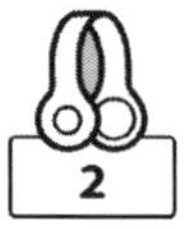

Middle C Blow

C is on the leger line below the Staff. A <u>Blow</u> note, 4th hole.

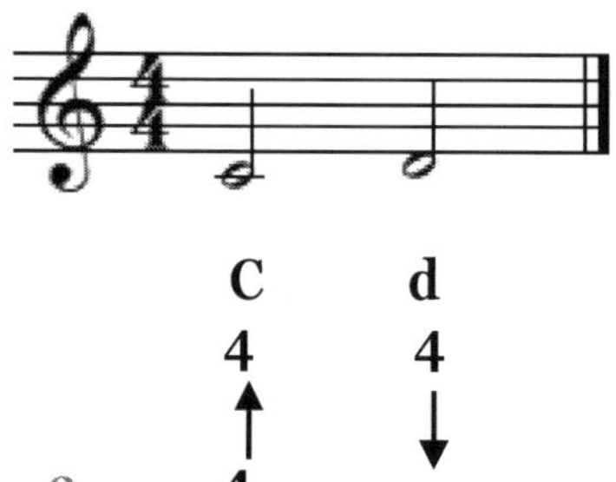

d draw

d is on the space below the staff. A <u>draw</u> note, 4th hole.

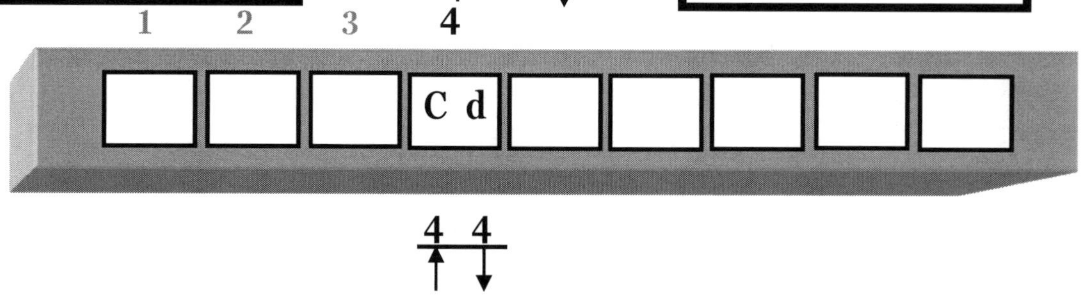

Whole note: o **= four (4) beats**

Half note: 𝅗𝅥 **= two (2) beats**

Threefold Amen

These Blow and draw notes (tones) are only in hole 4.

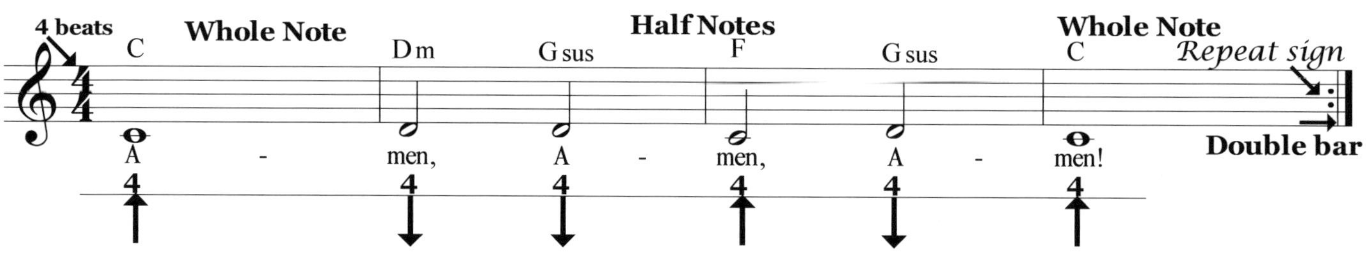

Quarter note: ♩ **= one (1) beat**

Alleluia!

♩ = 70

These Blow and draw notes (tones) are only in hole 4

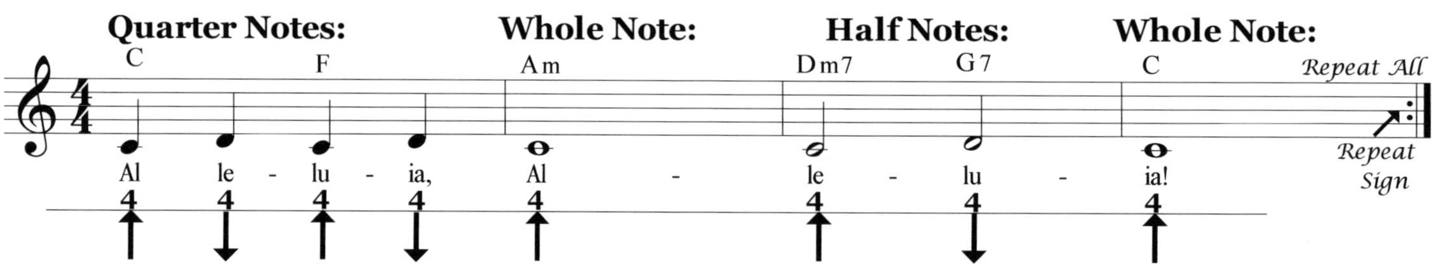

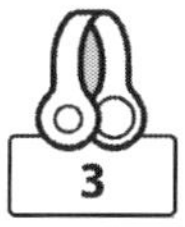

E **Blow**

E is on the 1ST line *(BOTTOM)* of the staff. A **Blow** note, 5th hole.

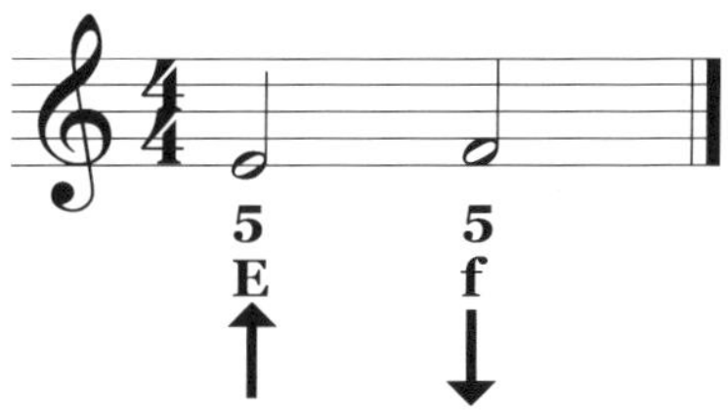

f **draw**

f is on the 1st space *(BOTTOM)* of the staff. A **draw** note, 5th hole.

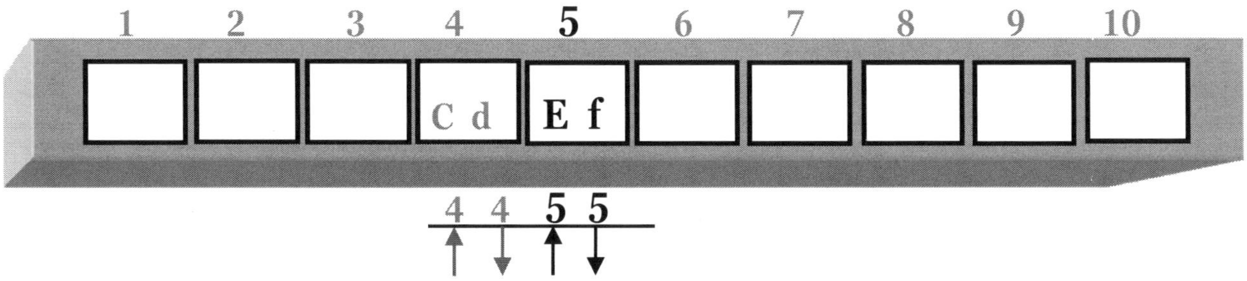

Counting (tapping) with your foot *(Downbeat/upbeat)*

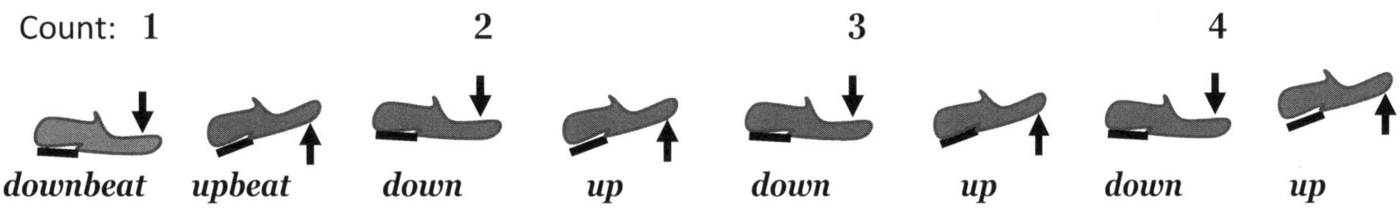

***Tempo* is the speed of the music or rhythm. ♩ = 70 indicates that quarter notes are played at a rate of 70 beats per minute. It is a good idea to use a metronome. It will help to keep the *tempo* even.**

Fivefold Amen

These Blow and draw notes (tones) are in holes 4 & 5.

♩ = 70

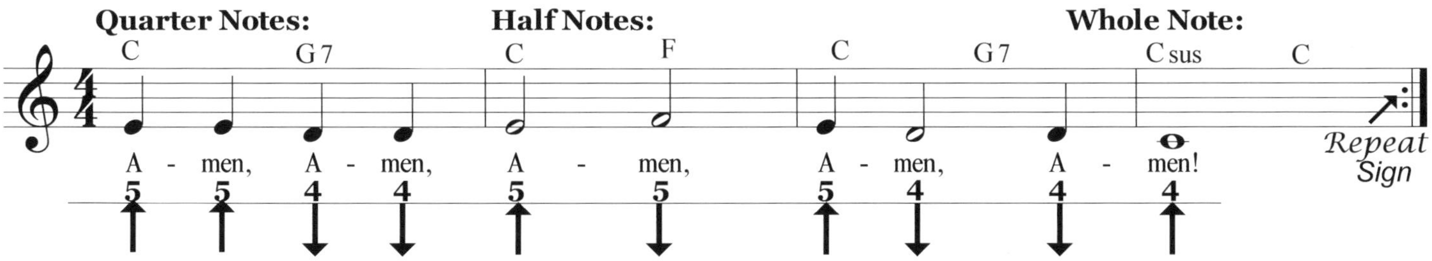

Slurred Notes: A curved line connecting two or more different pitches or tones.

Come, Christians Join to Sing

Christian Henry Bateman (1843) **Spanish Hymn (1824)**

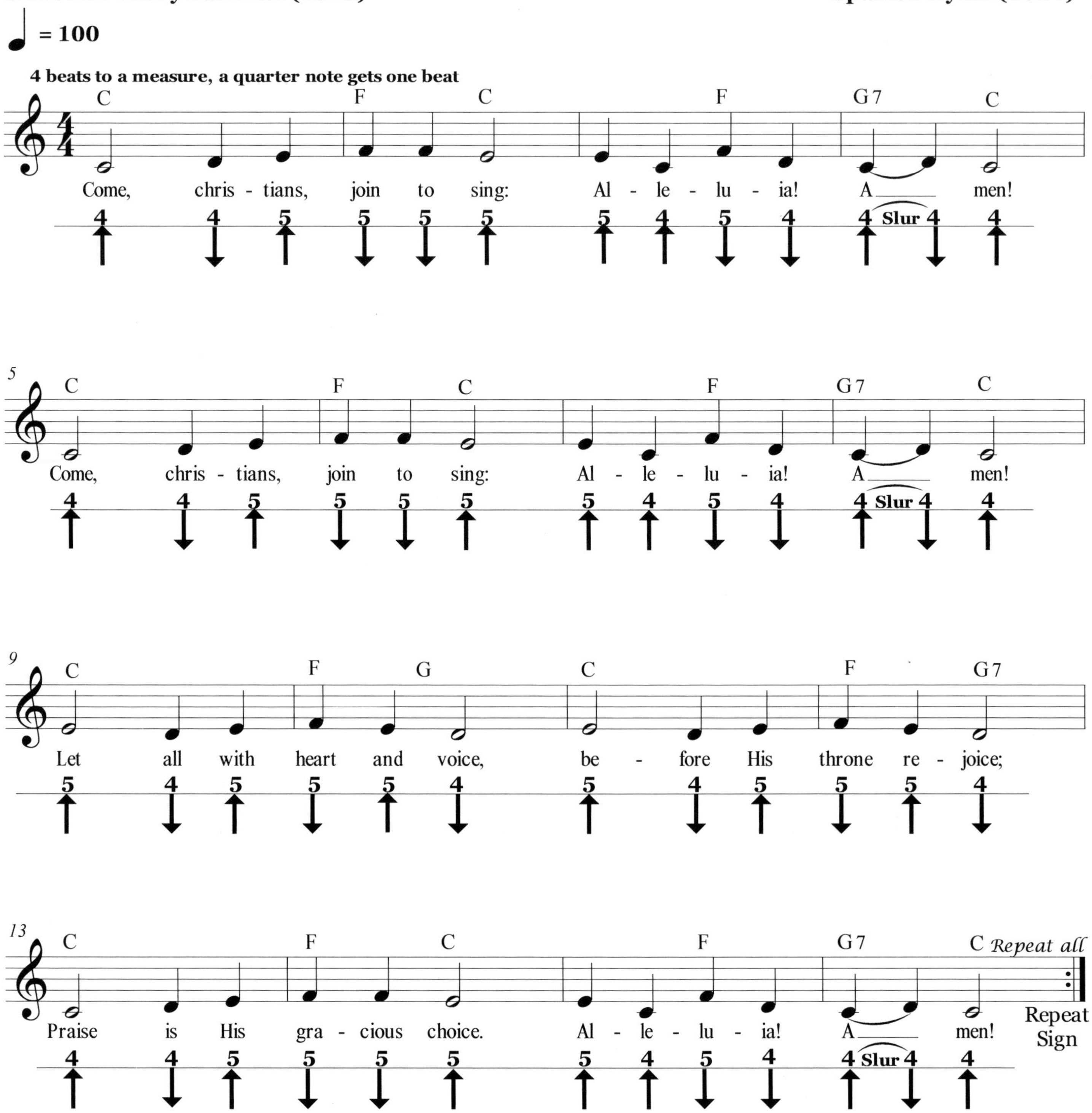

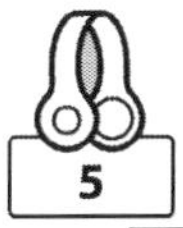

G Blow

G is on the second line of the staff. A **Blow** note, **6th hole.**

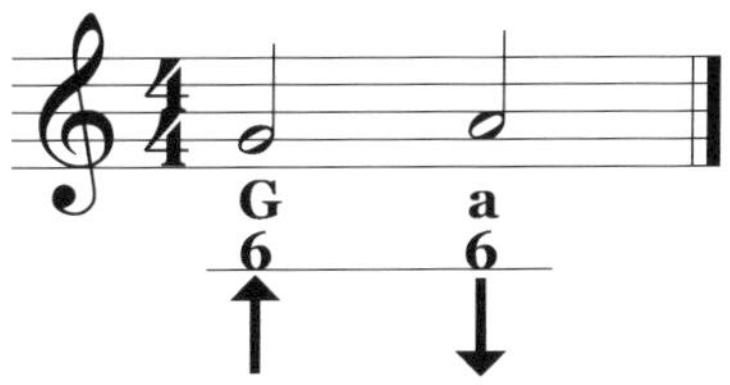

a draw

a is on the second space of the staff. A **draw** note, **6th hole.**

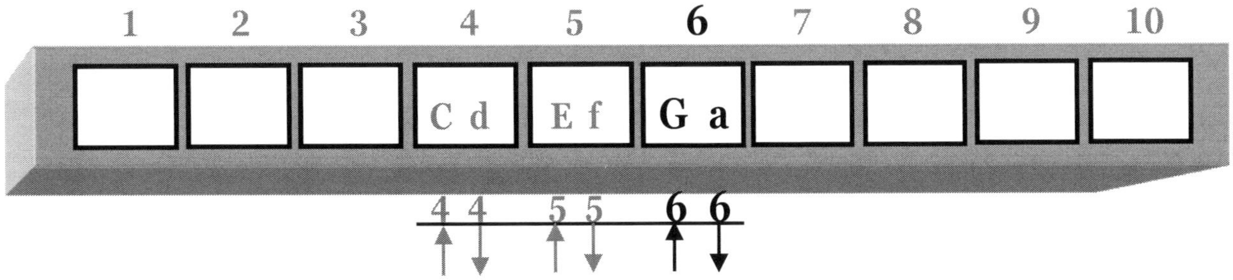

Dotted half note: 𝅗𝅥. = **3 beats**

𝅗𝅥 + ♩ = **3 beats**

God Is So Good

♩ = **110**

Anonymous

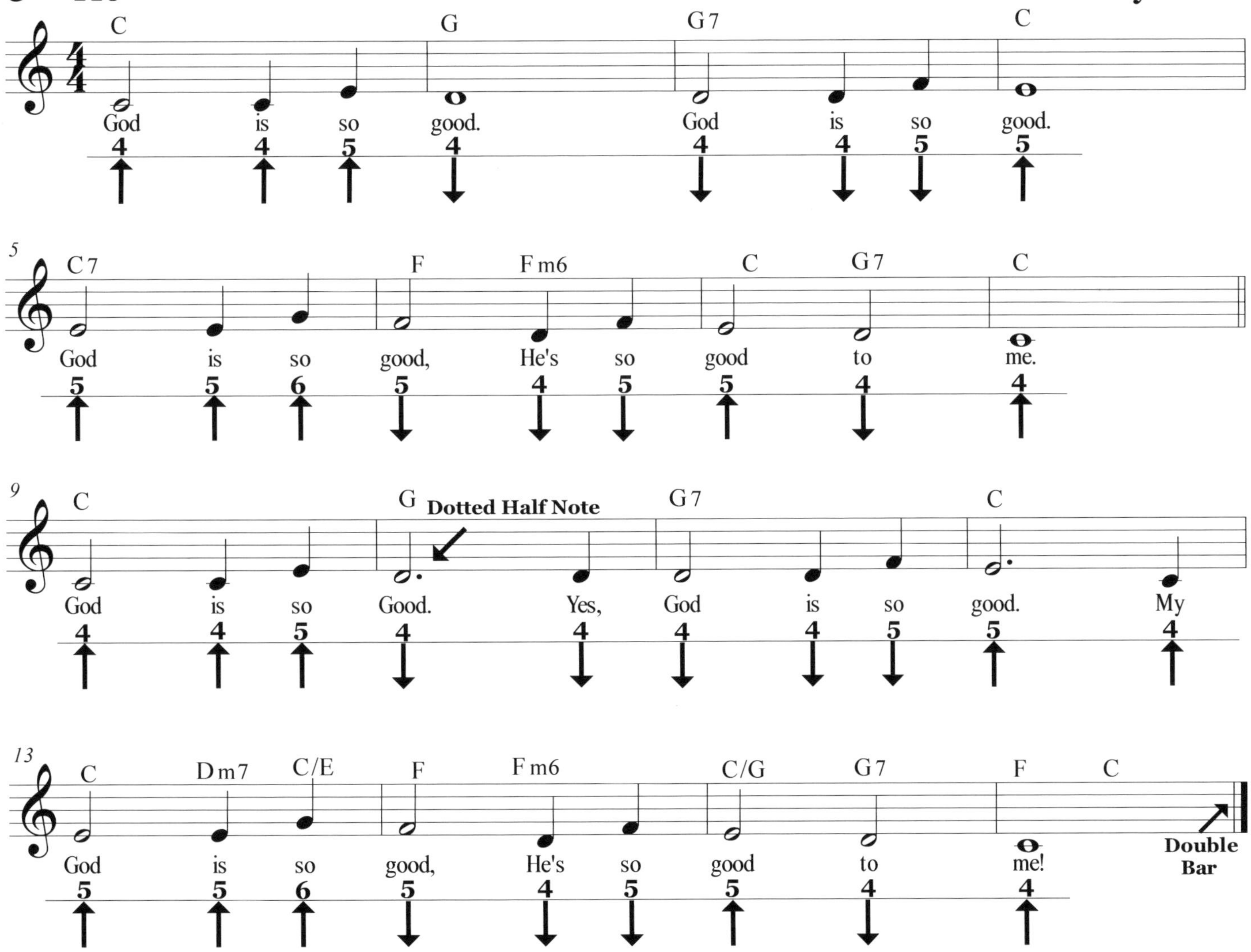

Here, O My Lord, I See Thee

Horatius Bonar (1857) **Edward Dearle (1874)**

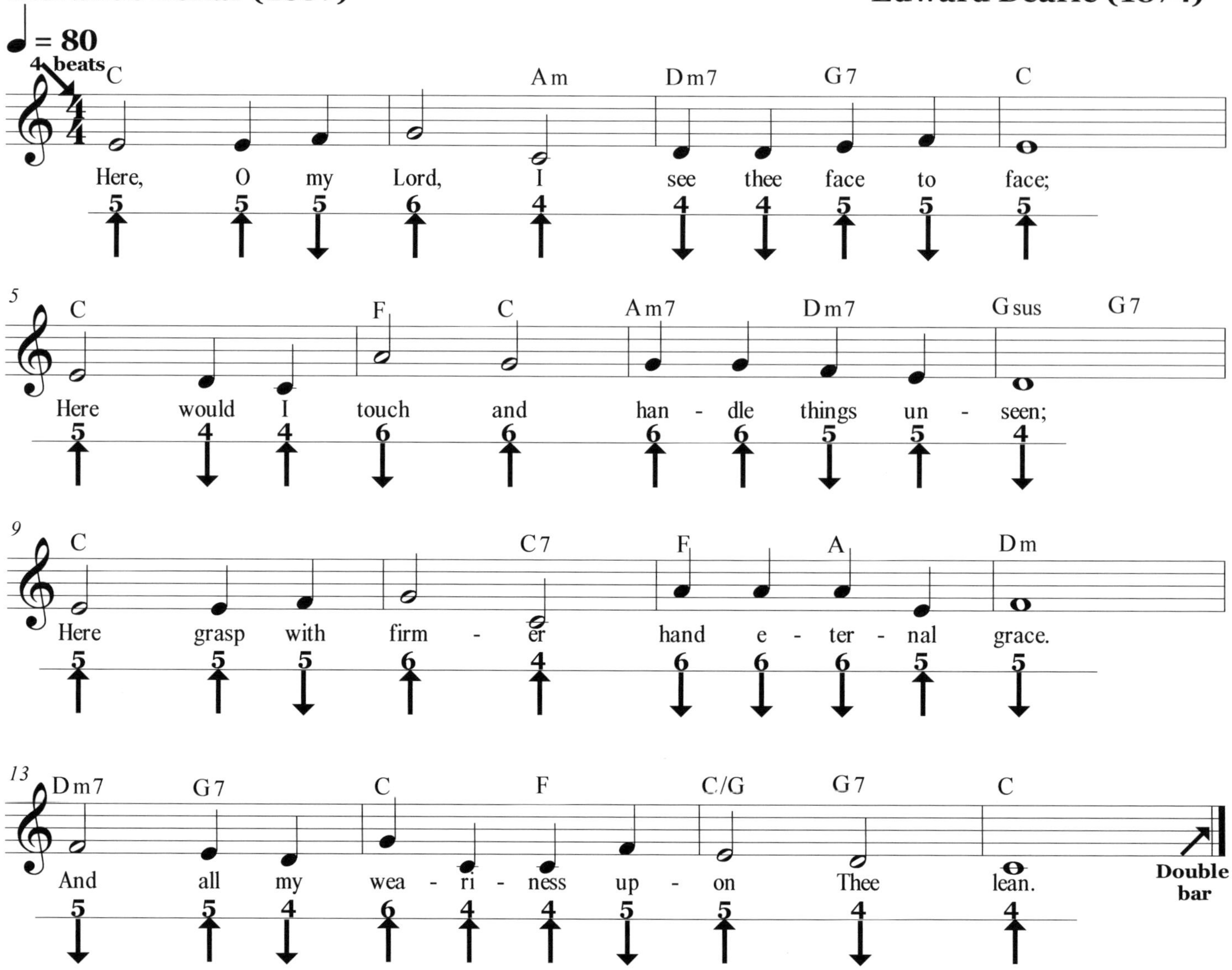

Time Signatures

Top number: 4 Number of beats per measure: 3, 2 (beats in a measure)

Bottom Number: 4 Kind of note that equals 1 beat: 4, 4 (Quarter note=1 beat)

Tied and Slurred Notes

1. Tied Notes: A curved line extends the length of the 1st pitch through the 2nd note of the same pitch.

2. Slurred Notes: Curved line connecting two or more different pitches or tones without attacking them separately. (Otherwards, try not to separate the two pitches)

8

2 = *Beats per measure*
4 = *Quarter note gets one beat*

When I Survey the Wondrous Cross

Isaac watts (1707) **Lowell Mason (1824)**

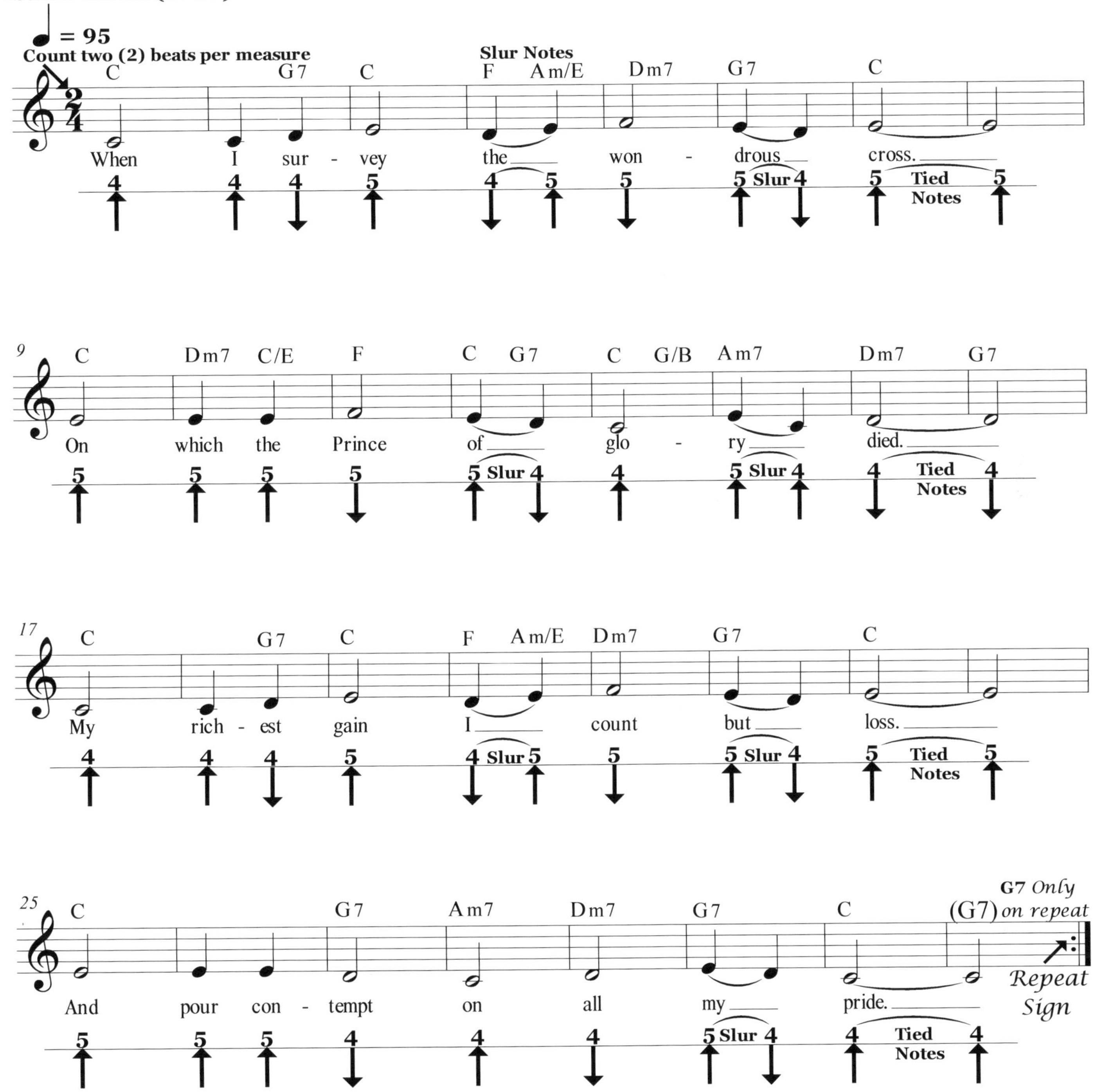

9

Dotted half note: 𝅗𝅥. = 3 beats   𝅗𝅥 + ♩ = 3 beats

Come, Sinners, to the Gospel Feast

Charles Wesley (1747)

Katholisches Gesangbuch (1774)

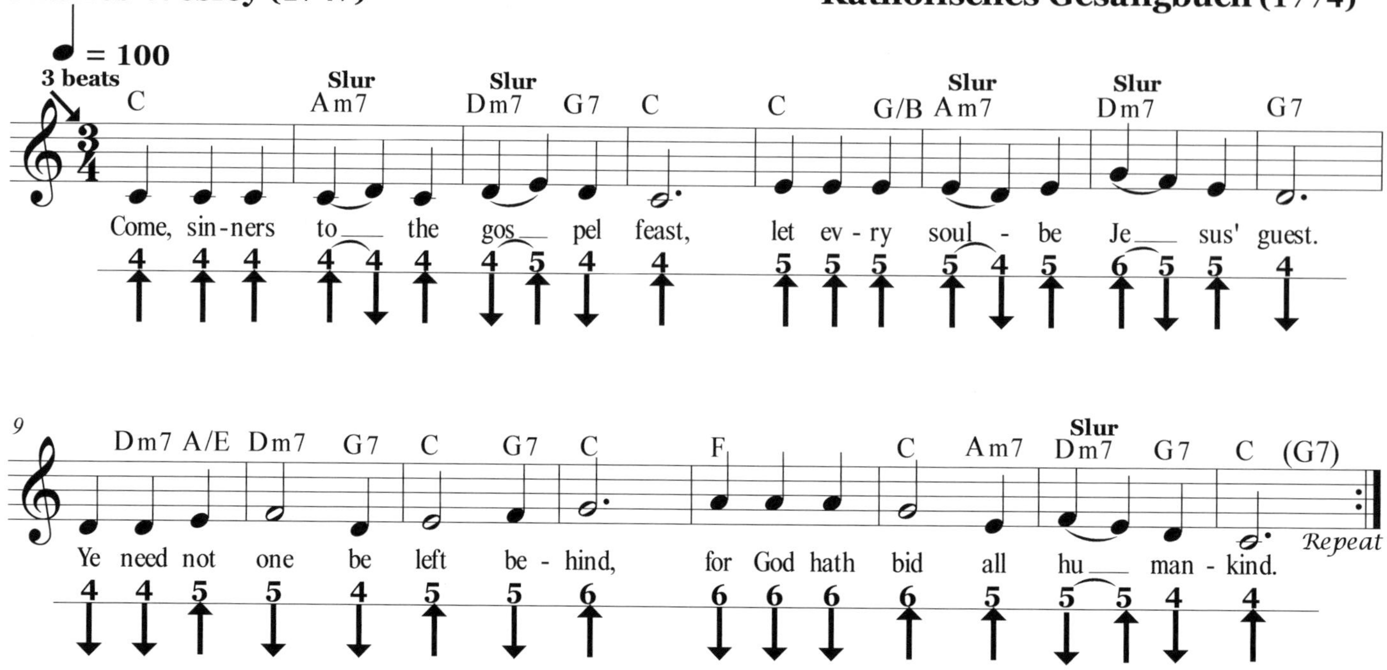

10

Fight the Good Fight

John S. B. Monsell (1863)

William Boyd (c. 1864)

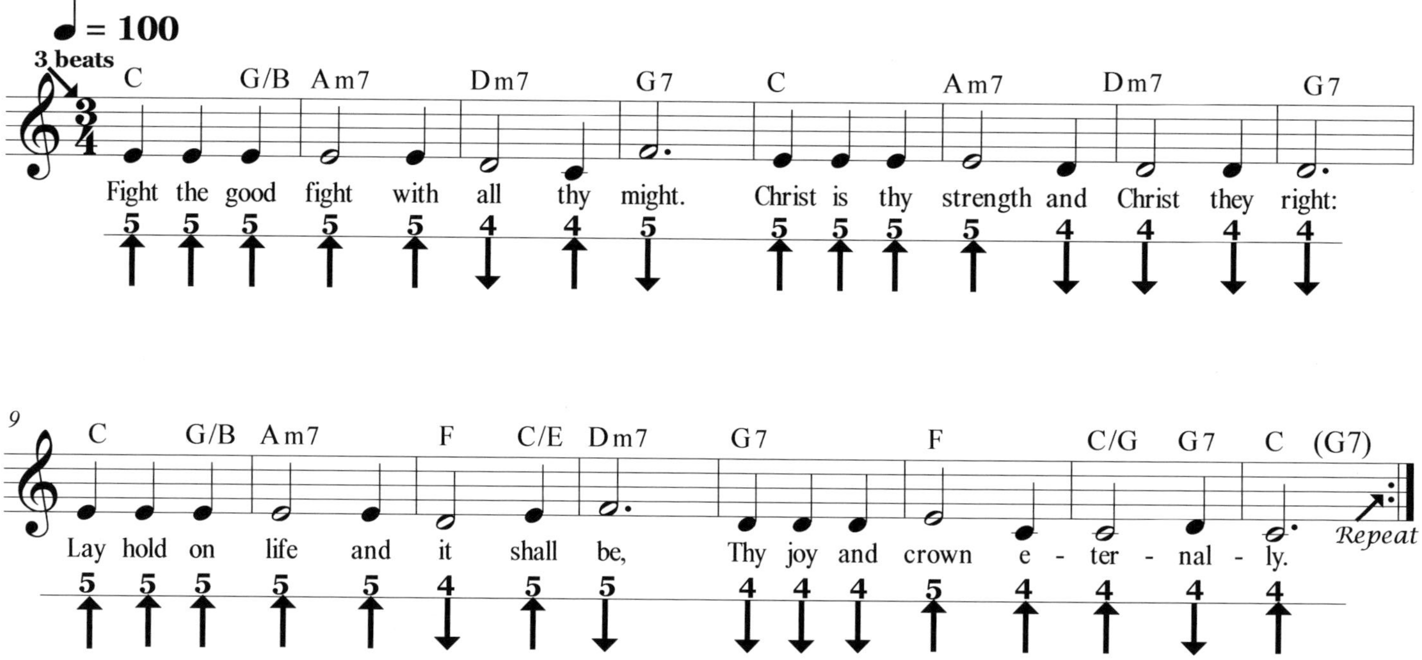

11

b draw

b is on the 3rd line of the staff. A **draw** note, 7th hole.

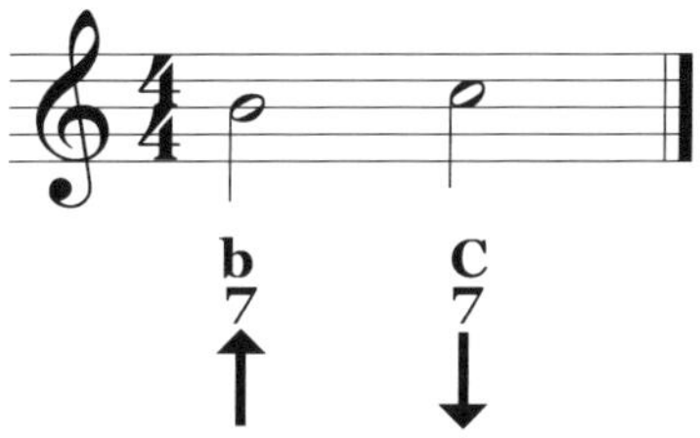

Full C Scale

High C Blow

C is on the 3rd Space of the staff. A **blow** note, 7th hole.

There are 8 notes **in the scale, the Blow-*draw* is reversed to *draw*-Blow in holes 7 to 10.**

Reversed: *draw*-Blow in hole 7

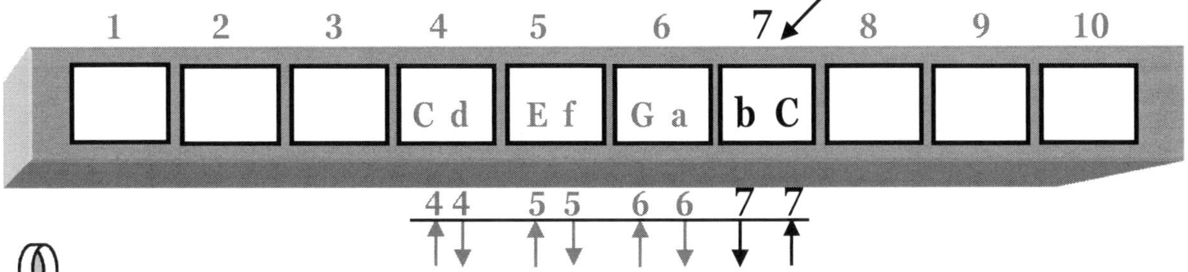

12

Break Thou the Bread of Life

Mary A. Lathbury (1877)

William F. Sherwin (1877)

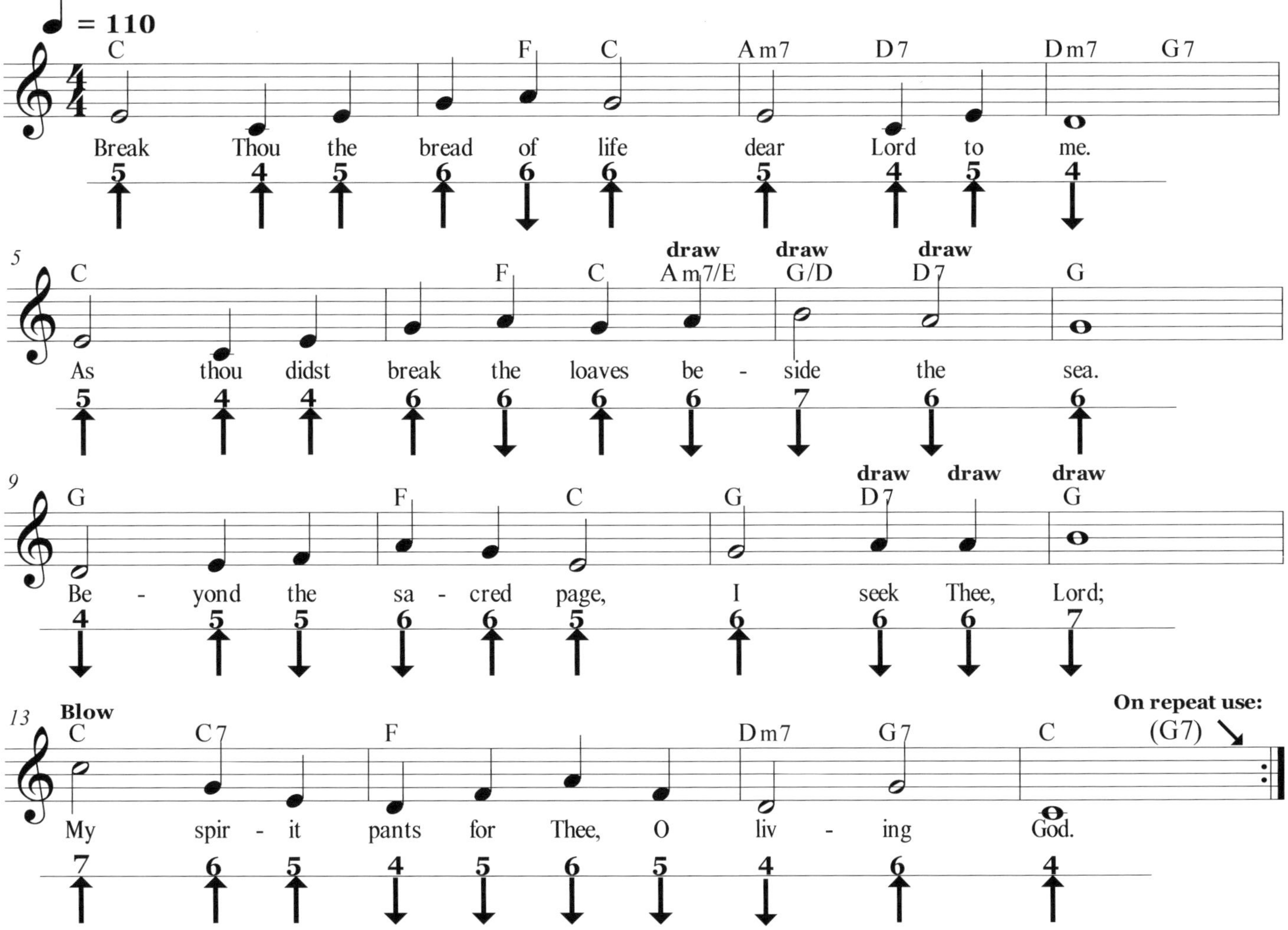

13

Anacrusis or "Pickup Notes"

A note or sequence of notes or a motif, which precedes the first downbeat in a full bar. Commonly known as "pickup notes", an unstressed lead-in of a note or notes.

Rests – Silence is an equally important part of the music.

1. **Quarter (¼) Rest = one (1) beat** 𝄽 ***silent* for one (1) beat**
2. **Half (½) Rest = two (2) beats** 𝄼 ***silent* for two (2) beats**

How Sweet the Name of Jesus Sounds

John Newton (1779) **Alexander R. Reinagle** (1799-1877)

♩ = 80

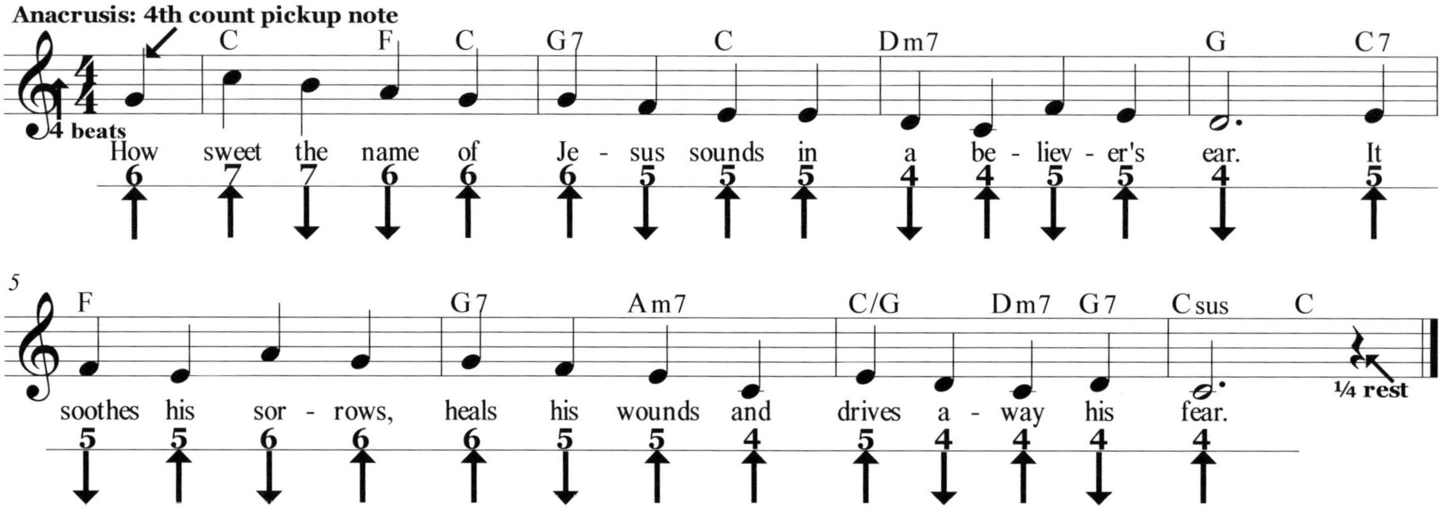

14

Breathe on Me, Breath of God

Edwin Hatch (1878) **Robert Jackson** (1888)

♩ = 100

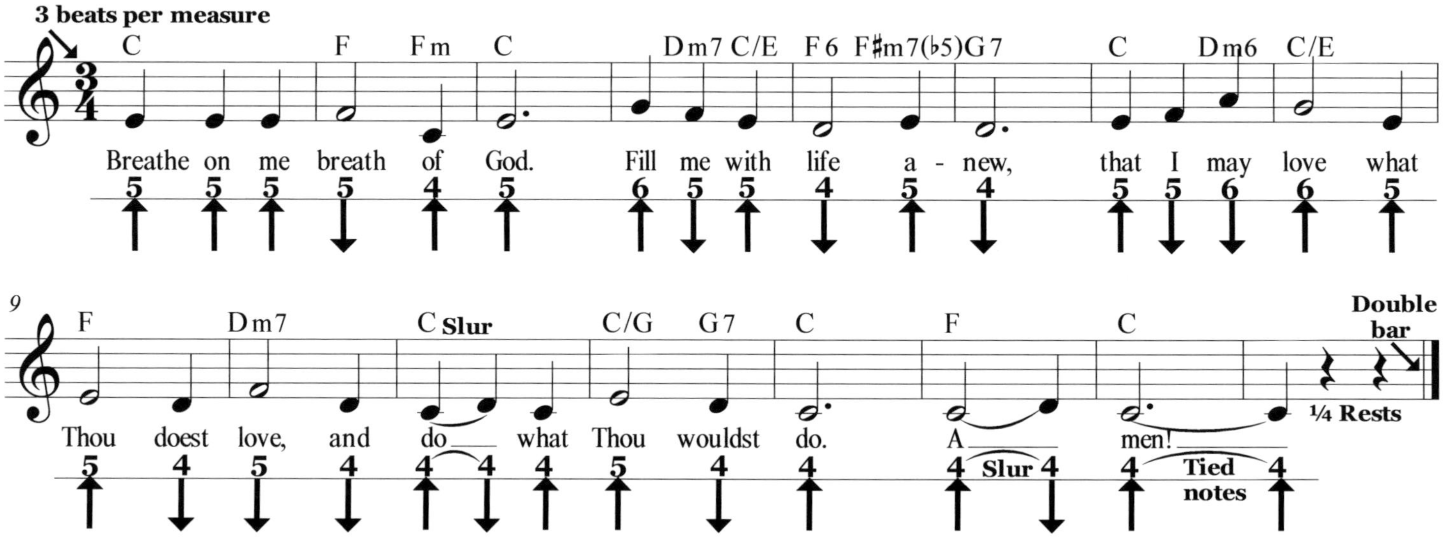

1st and 2nd endings were created to shorten the printing of music. The repeat sign indicates a return to the repeat sign, repeat, then skip 1st ending, play the 2nd ending, concluding at the word *fine*.

15

Be Still and Know that I Am God

Psalm 46:10 **Anonymous**

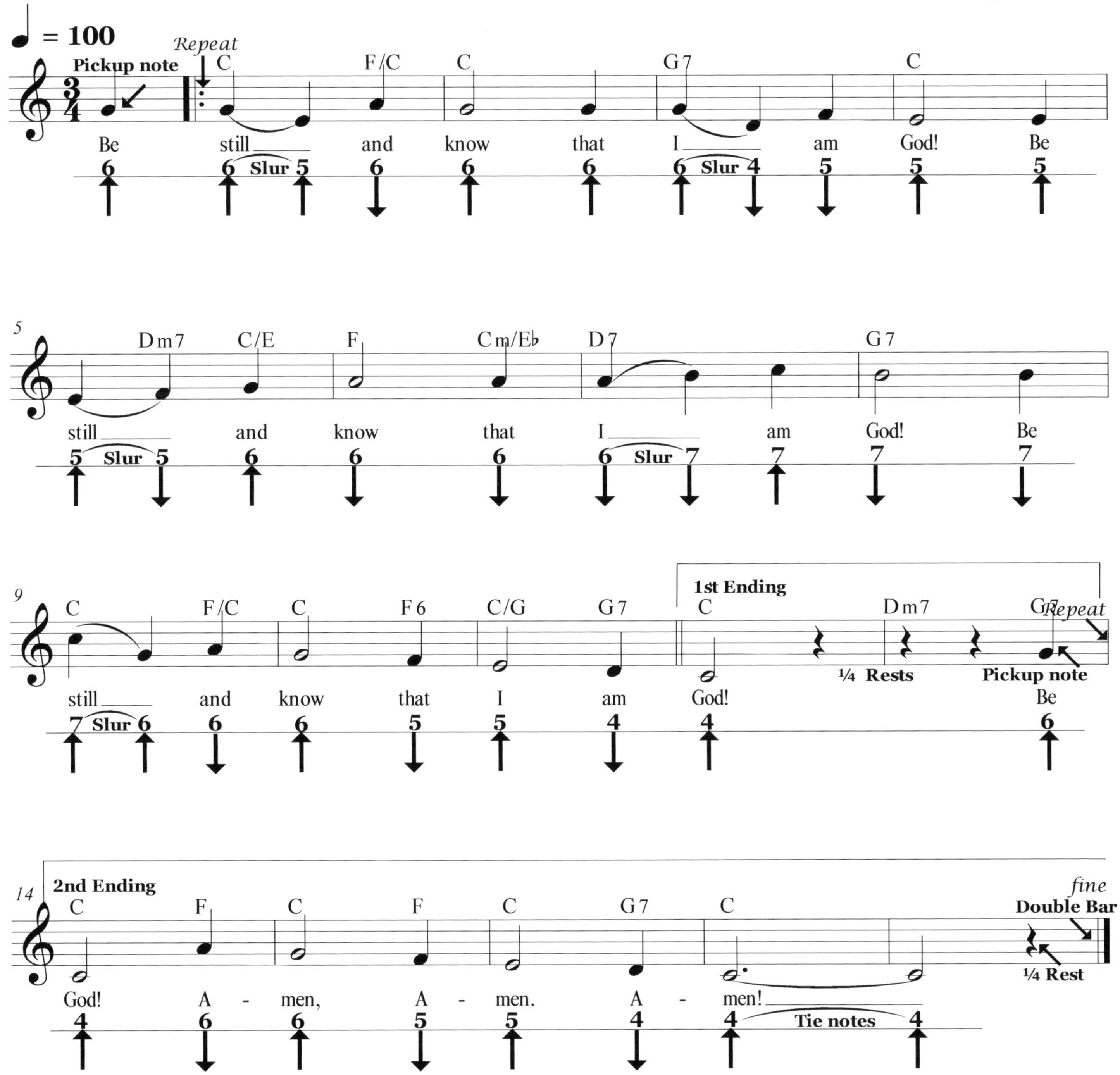

Eighth Notes

Eighth notes: ♪ = one-half (½) **beat; Eight** (8) **eighth notes per measure.**

It takes two (2) eighth notes: ♪ + ♪ = to equal one (1) **quarter note.**

Dotted quarter notes = ♩. (1½ beats) **♩. + ♪ = 2 beats** (1½ + ½ = 2 beats)

Dotted quarter notes are counted as shown below:

1 & 2 & 3 & 4 &

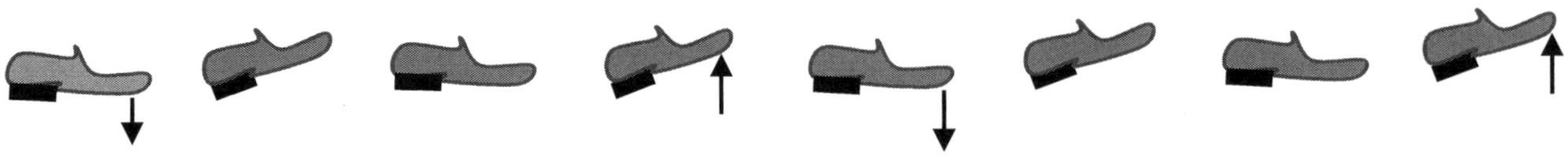

♩. = 1 ½ beats ♪ = ½ ♩. = 1 ½ beats ♪ = ½

Come Into His Presence (4-part Canon)

Psalm 100:2

Round For 4 Players

4 players - repeat 4 times:

1st player **begins,**
2nd player **begins when 1st player gets to the 2nd bar,**
3rd player **begins when the 2nd player gets to the 2nd bar,**
4th player **begins when the 3rd player gets to the 2nd bar.**
All players play this 4 times.

♩ = 70 **Traditional**

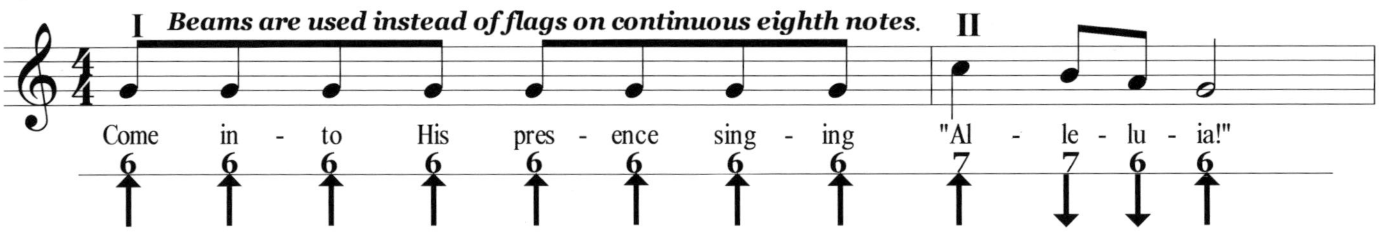

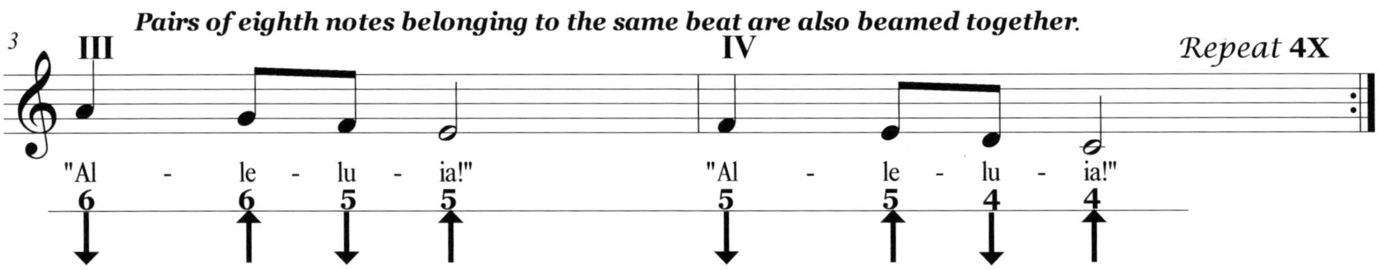

To Be Like Jesus

♩ = 80

Traditional

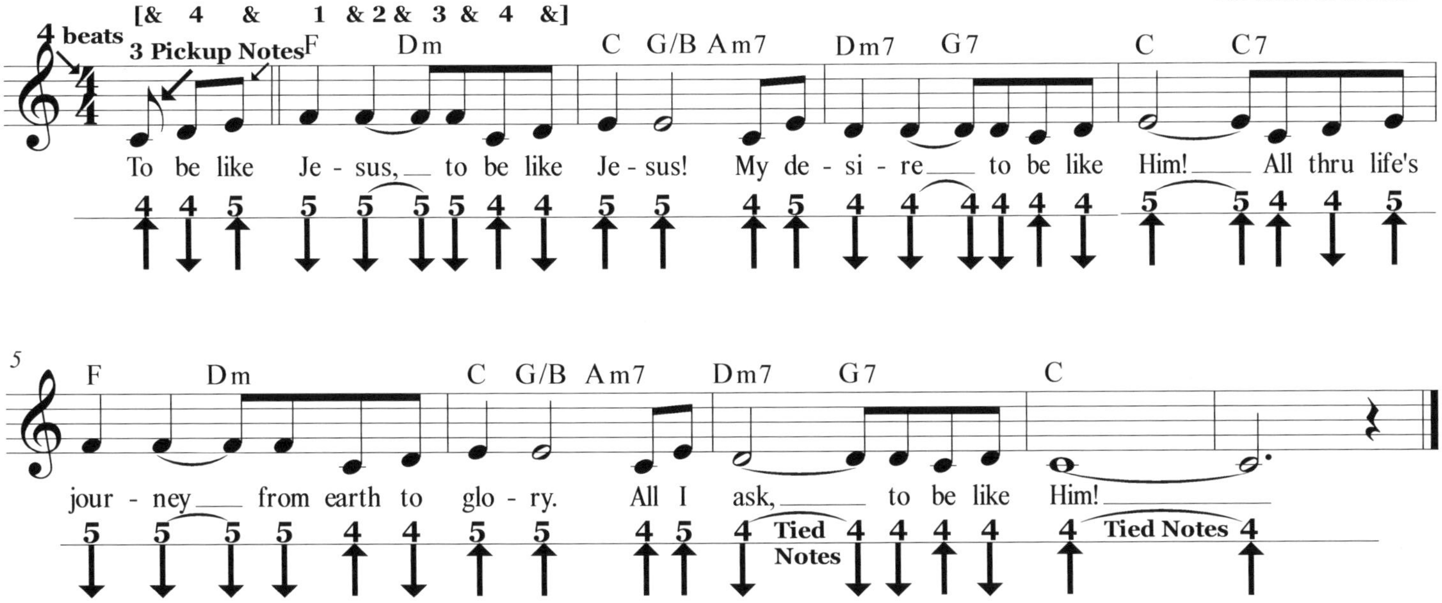

Reminder: 1st and 2nd endings and *D.C. al fine* are used. Da Capo or "*D.C.*" means to the beginning, "*al fine*" means to the end (*fine*). Return to the repeat sign at the beginning, repeat, then skip 1st ending, play the 2nd ending, concluding at the word *fine*.

A Child of the King

Harris E. Buell (1898) **John B Sumner** (1900)

♩ = 85

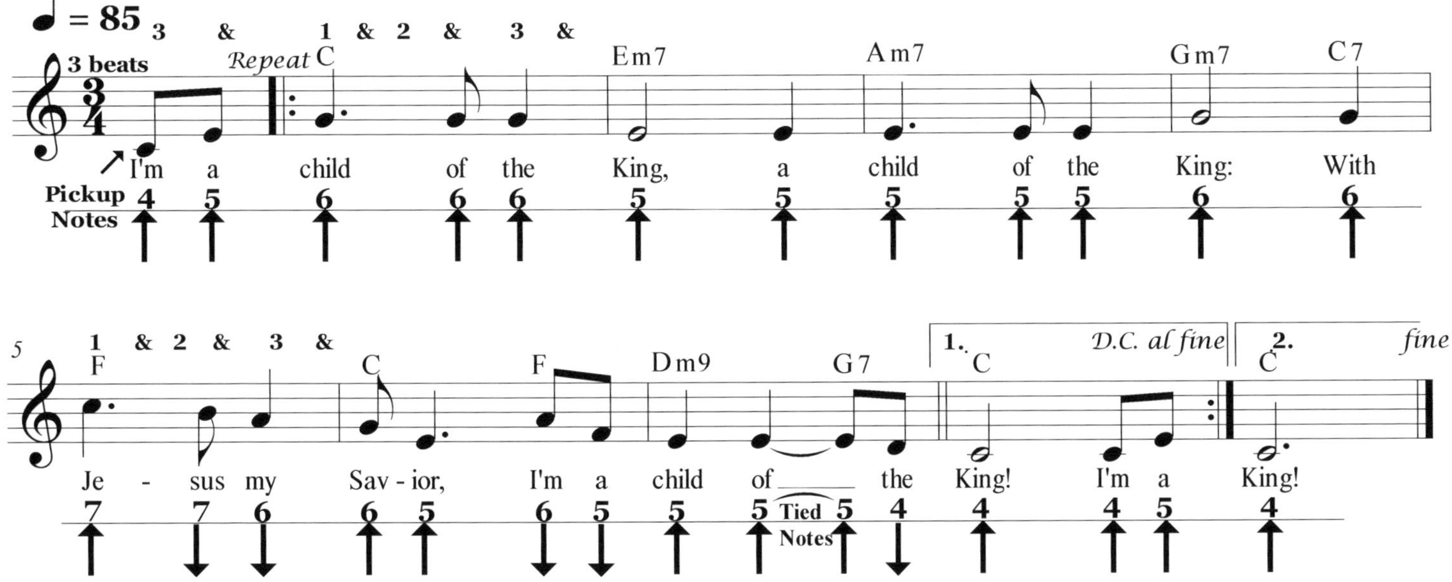

19

Trust and Obey

John H. Sammis (1887) **Daniel B. Towner (1887)**

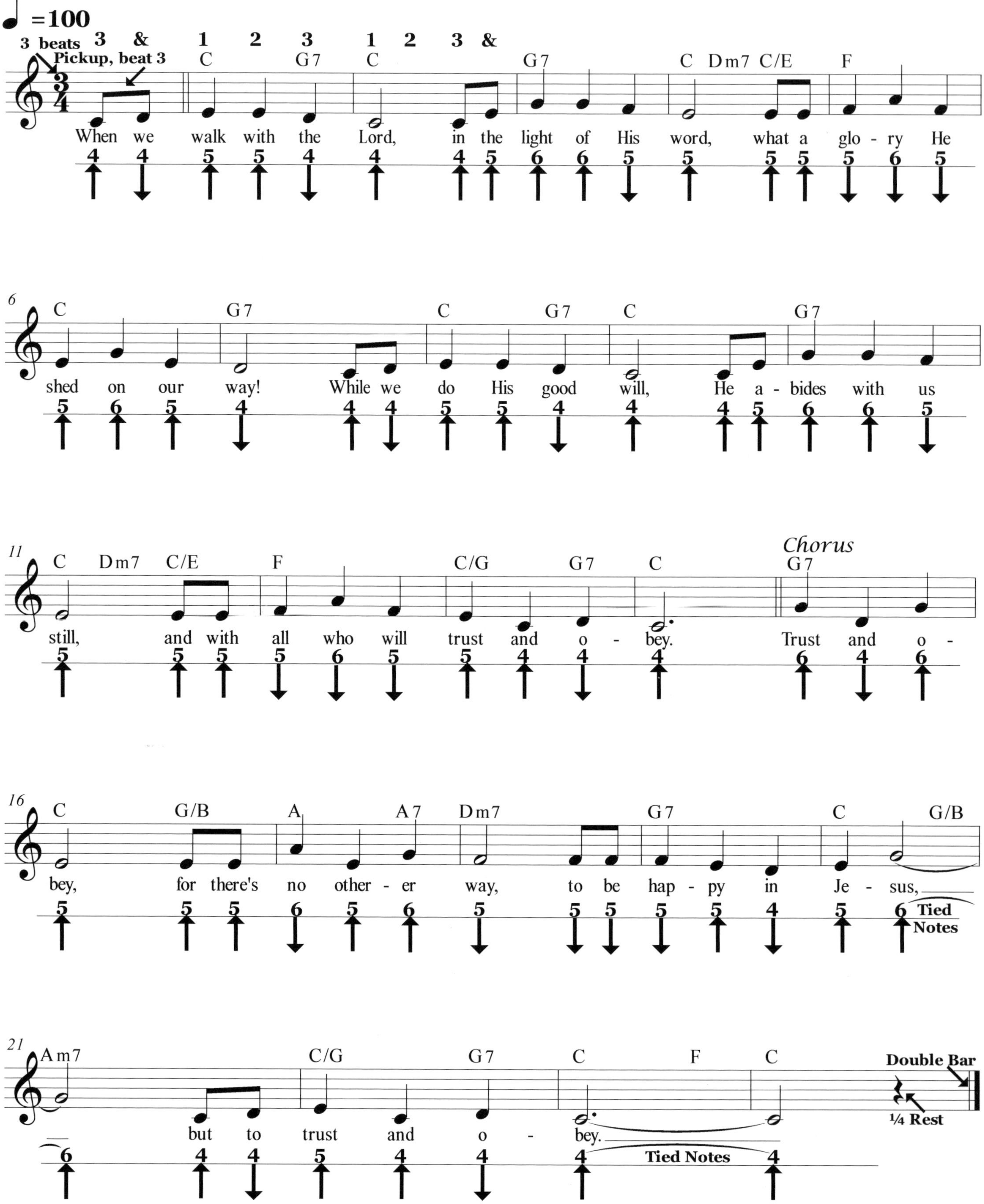

20

Dotted Quarter Note: ♩. = 1 ½ Counts

I Surrender All

Reverently

J. W. Van Deventer (1896) **W. S. Weeden (1896)**

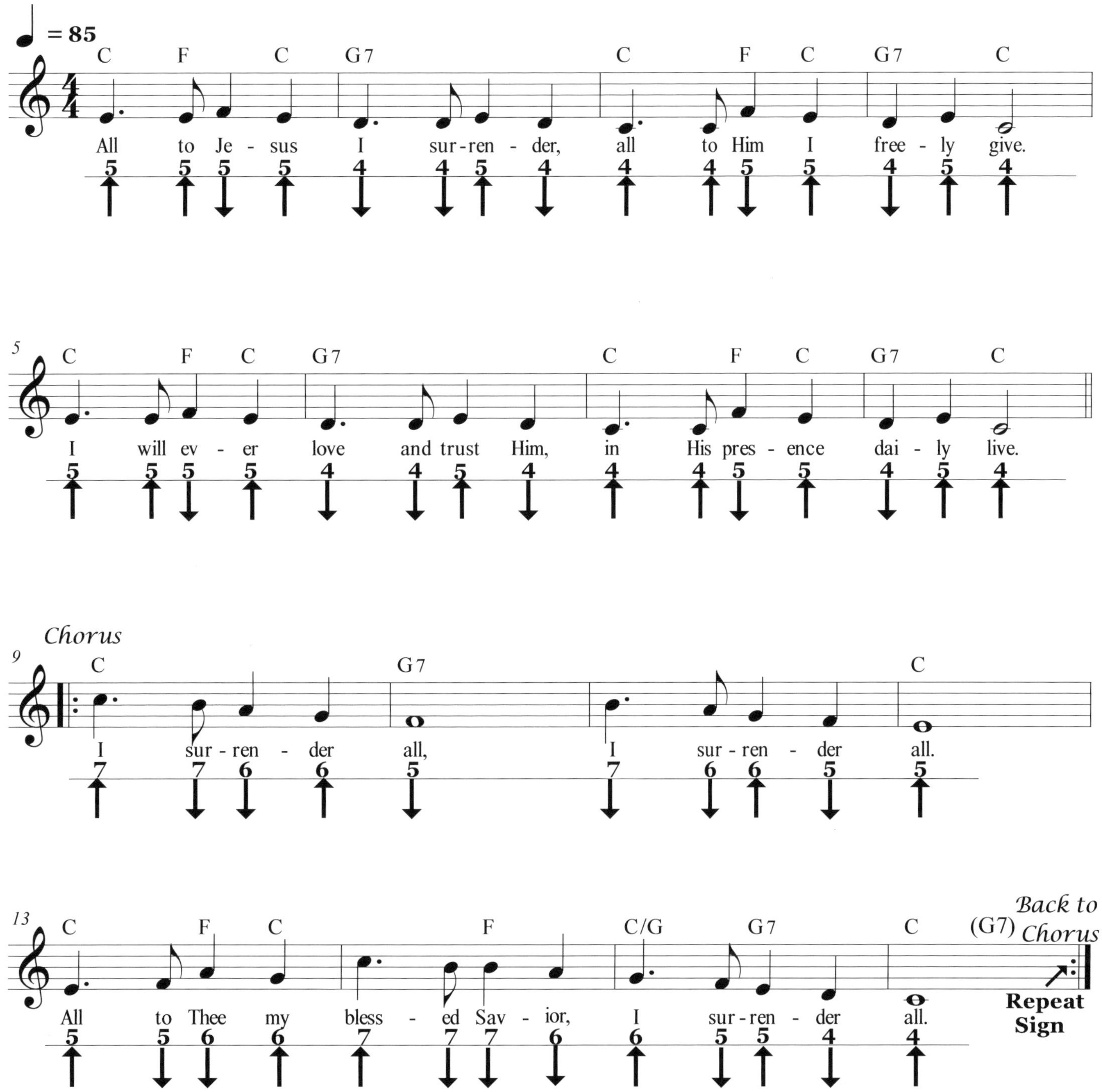

Savior, Like a Shepherd, Lead Us (*Blessed Jesus*)

Dorothy A. Thrupp (1836) **William B. Bradbury** (1859)

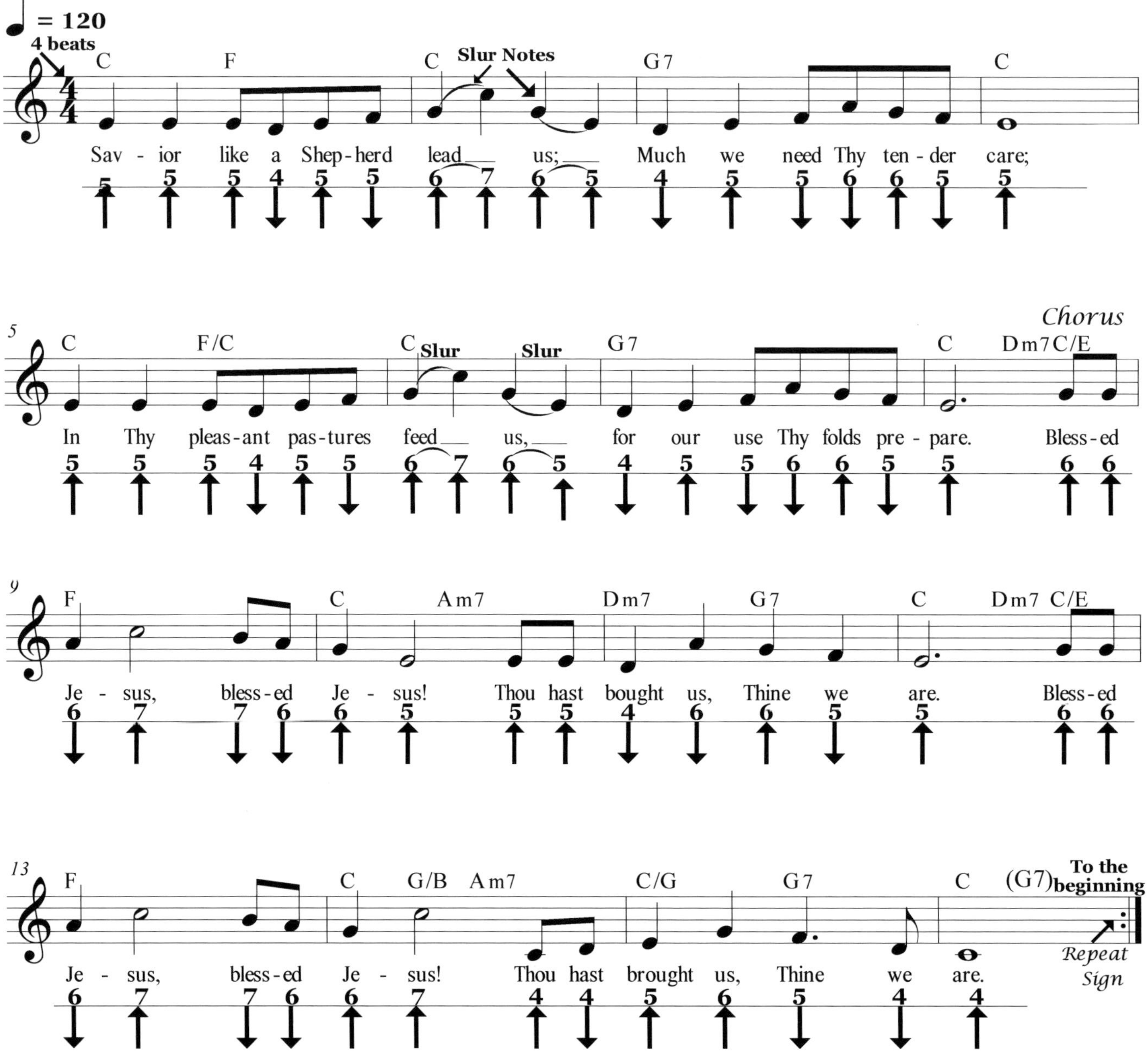

Low b

Low b is below the staff,
Under the 1st leger line,
a **draw** note, **3rd** hole.

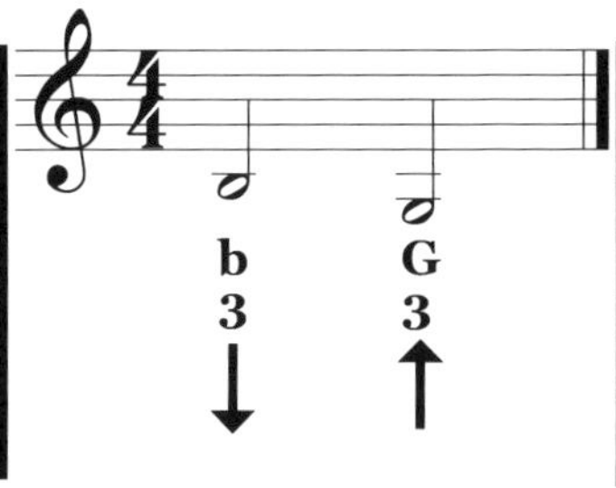

Low G

Low G is below the staff,
below the 2nd Leger line,
a **Blow** note, **3rd** hole.

Notice: There is no **"A"** note in the lower register of the instrument.
This is due to the Richter tuning of the diatonic harmonica.

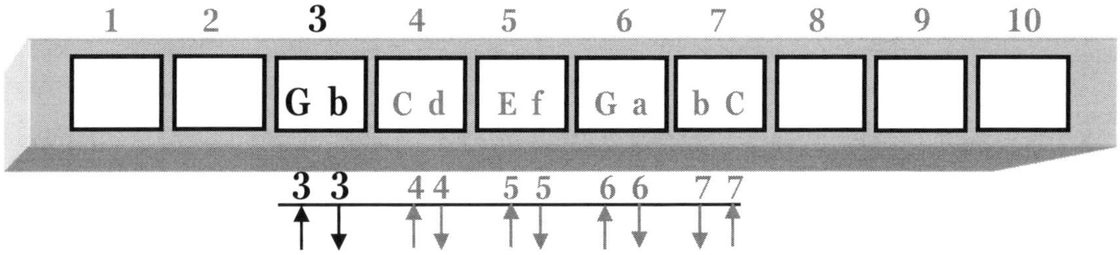

Psalm 85:7 & 126:3

Adapt. Old English Melody **Leisentritt's Gesangbuch (1567)**

♩ = 95

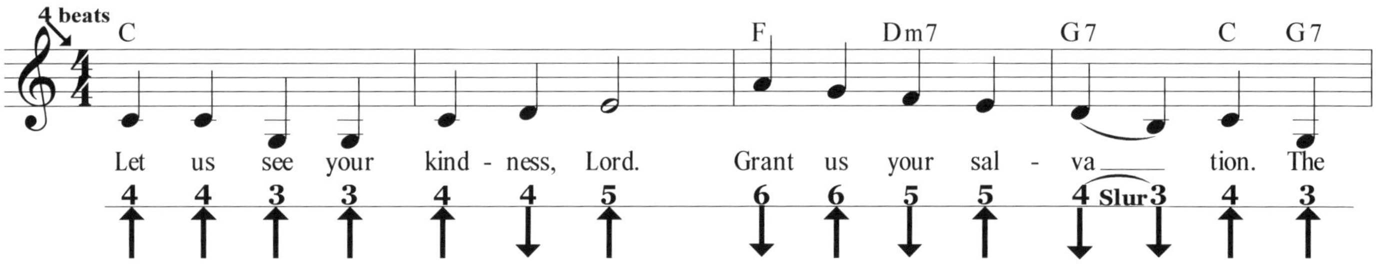

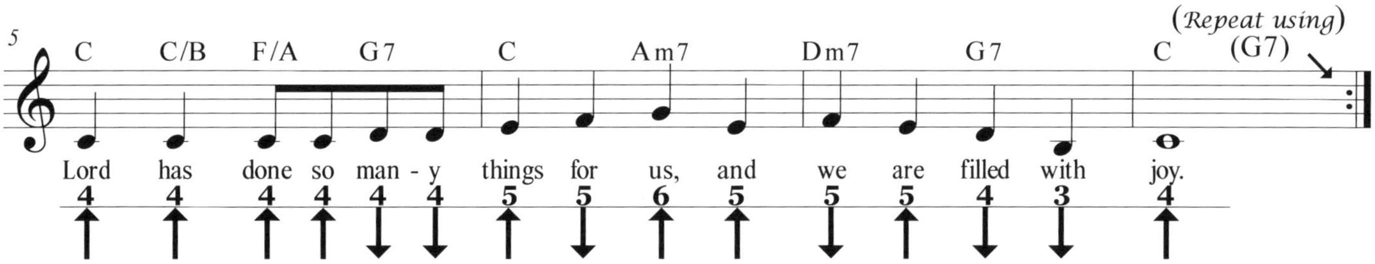

23

O Come, Let Us Adore Him

Traditional **Wade's Cantus Diversi (1751)**

♩ = 95

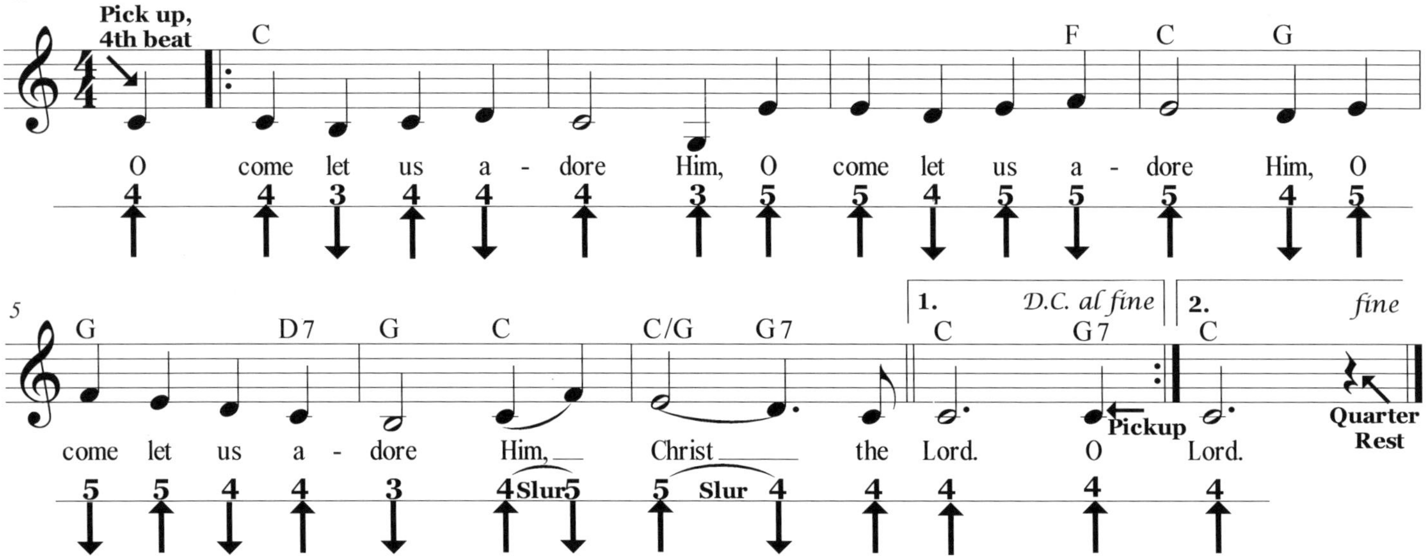

24

Angels We Have Heard on High

Multi-note slurs played legato style

♩ = 120 **Traditional French Carol**

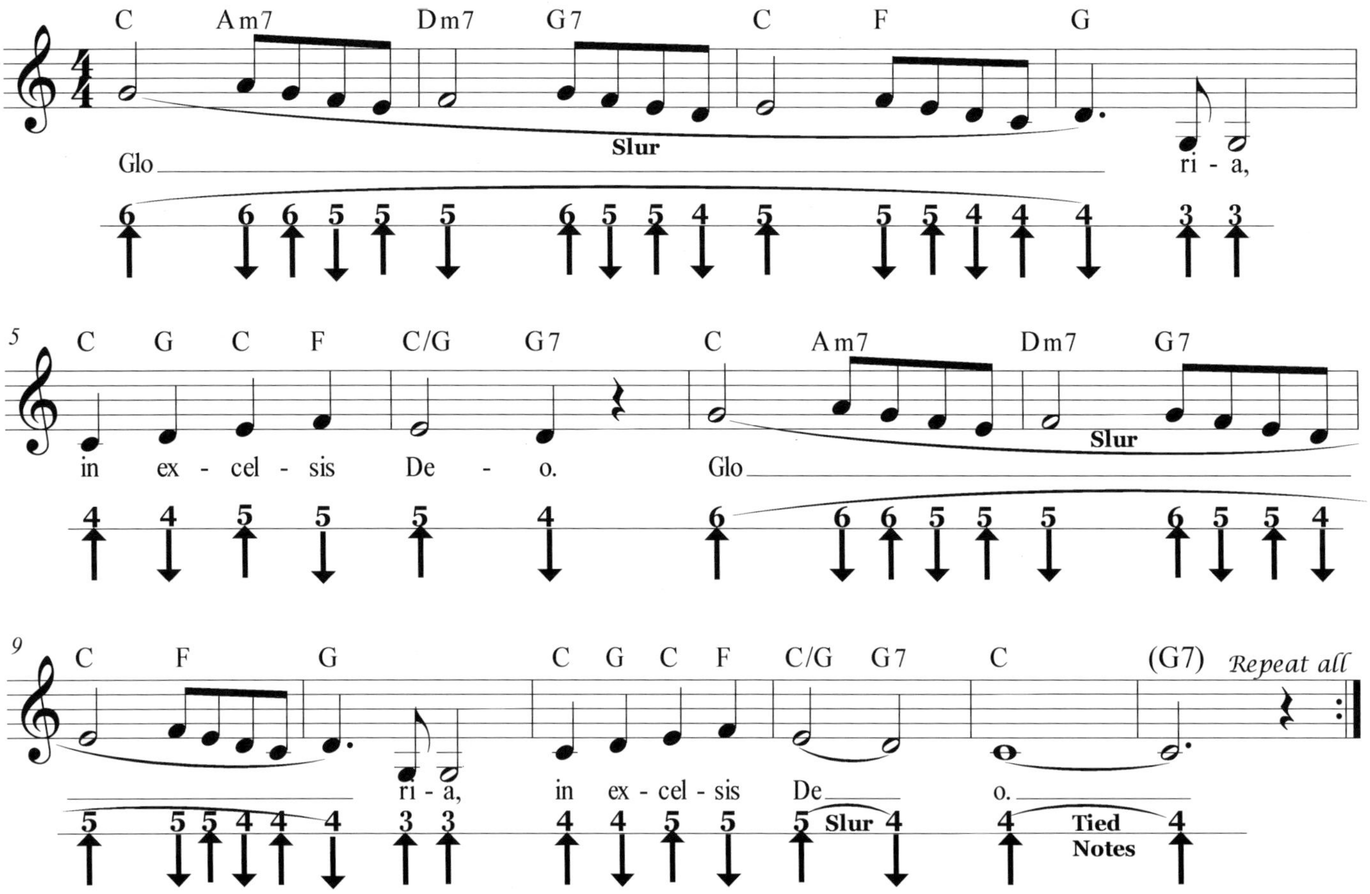

My Jesus, I Love Thee

William R. Featherston (1864) **Adoniram J. Gordon (1864)**

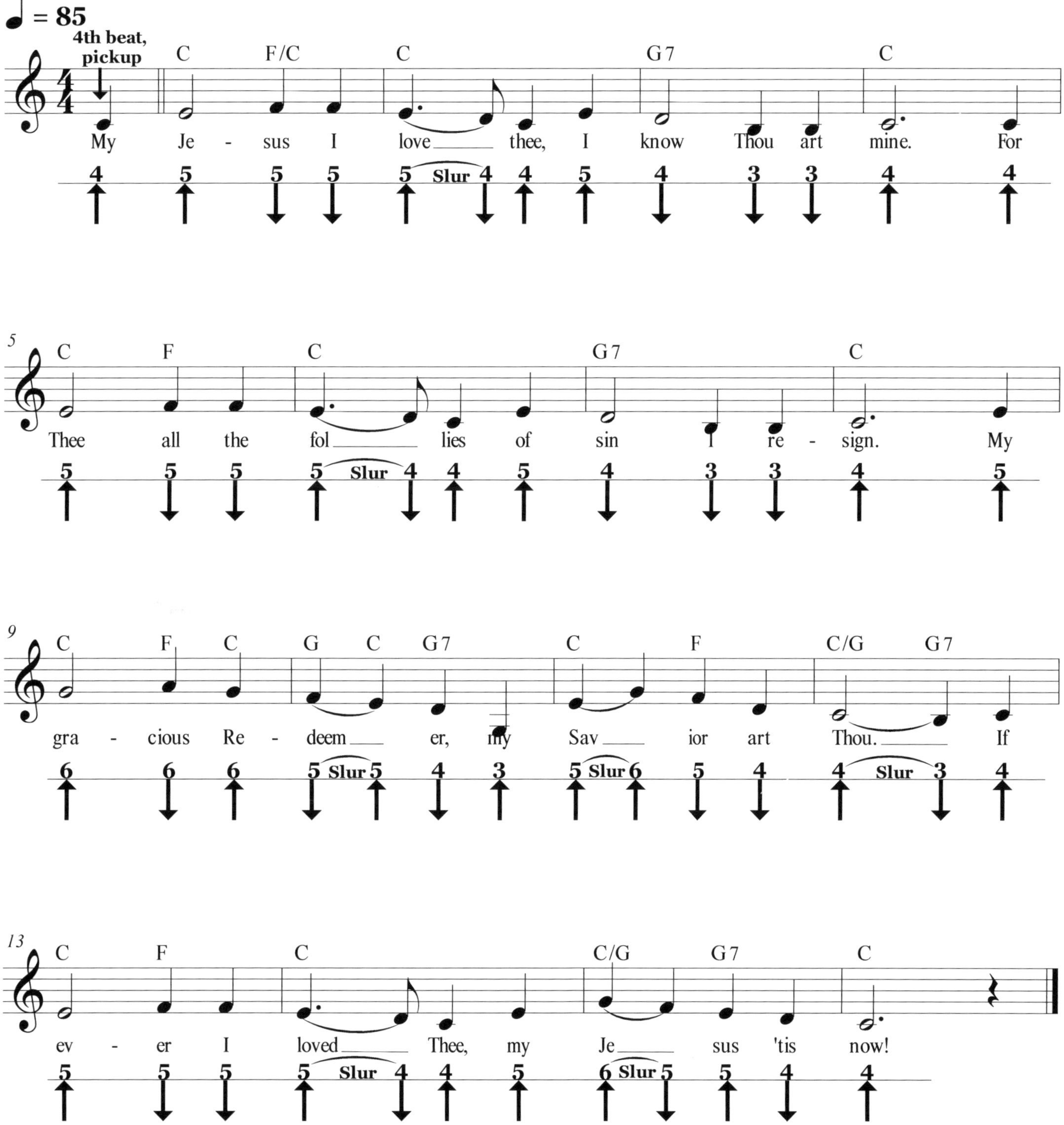

26

The Solid Rock (My Hope Is Built)

Edward Mote (1834) **William B. Bradbury (1863)**

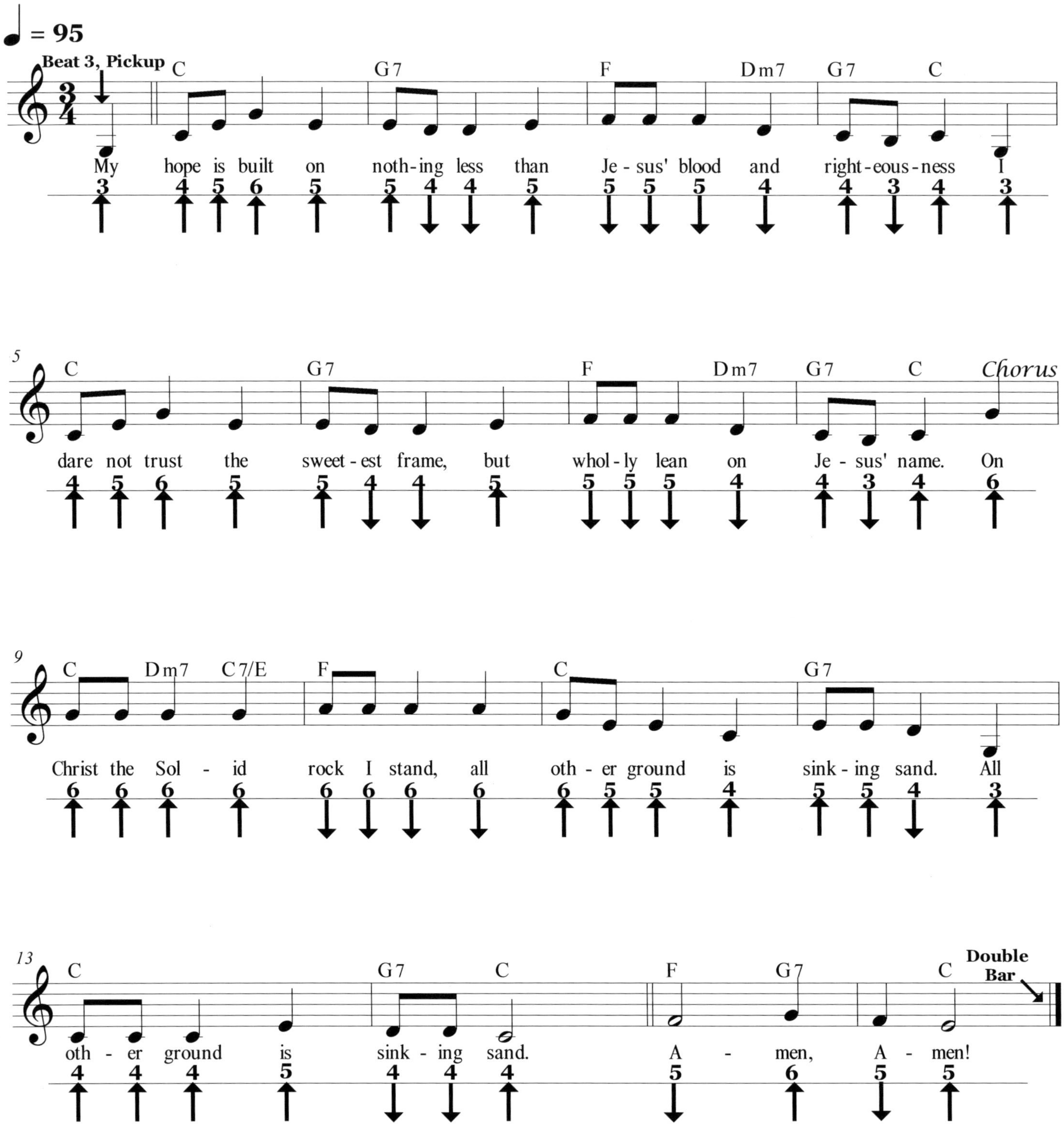

27

Come Bless the Lord

Psalm 134:1, 2

Anacrusis in every other measure!

Anonymous

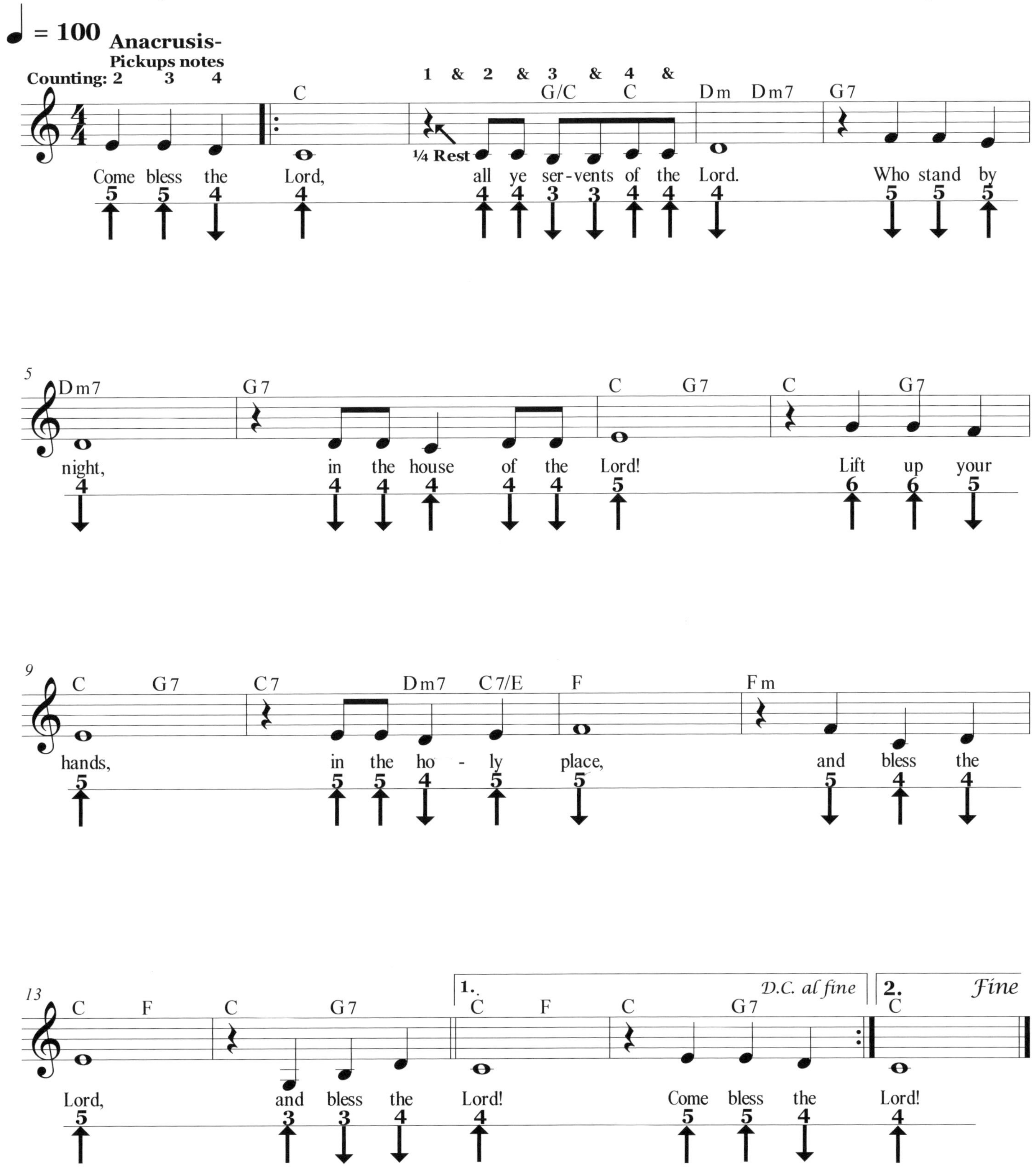

28

Dal Segno *D.S. al fine*: **From the sign 𝄋. A direction of repetition from the sign.** *al fine* **to the end. Go back to the sign then proceed to the 2nd ending** *(fine)* **skipping the 1st ending.**

Close to Thee

Fanny J. Crosby, 1874 **Silas J. Vail, 1874**

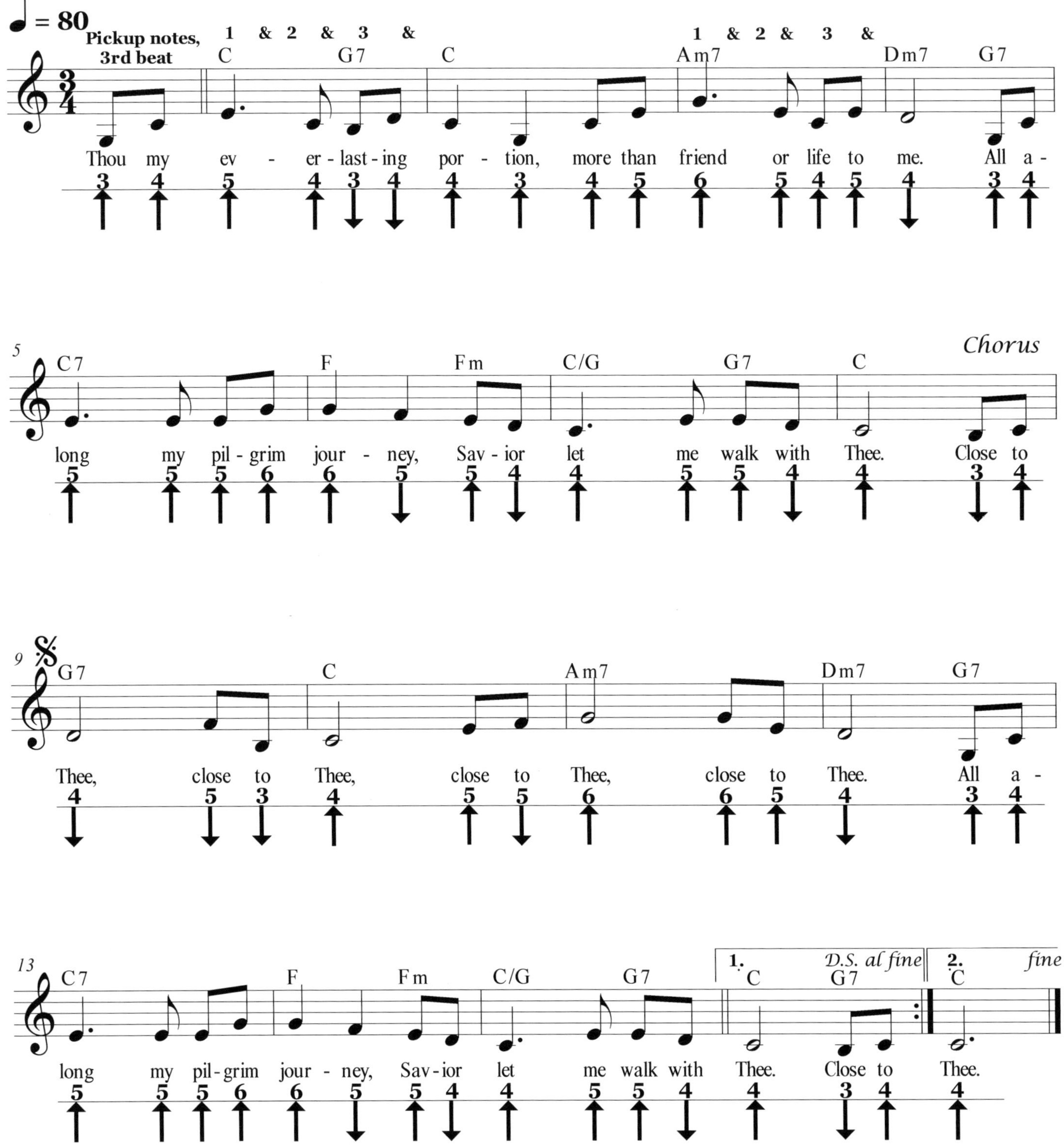

High d

d is on the 4th line of the staff. A **draw** note, 8th hole.

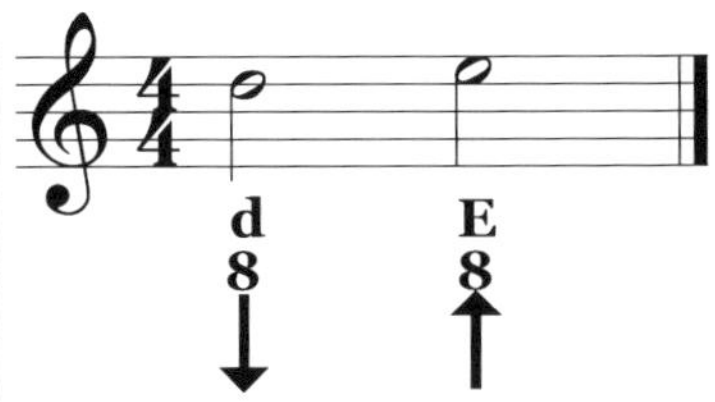

High E

E is on the 4th space of the staff. A **Blow** note, 8th hole.

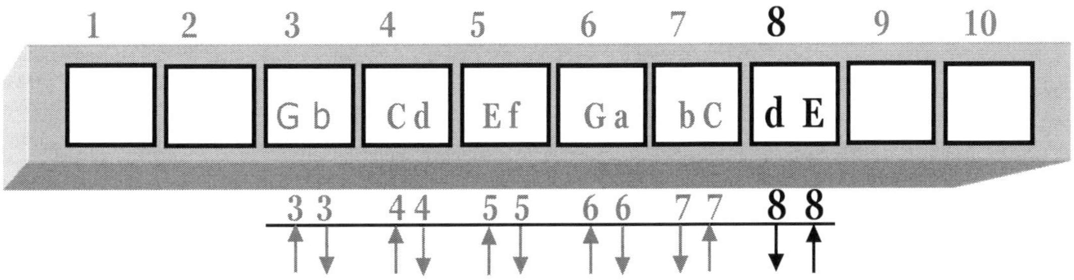

Bless the Lord, O My Soul

(*Repeat* **twice (2x) then play again to the 3rd ending to** *fine*)

♩ = 90

Anonymous

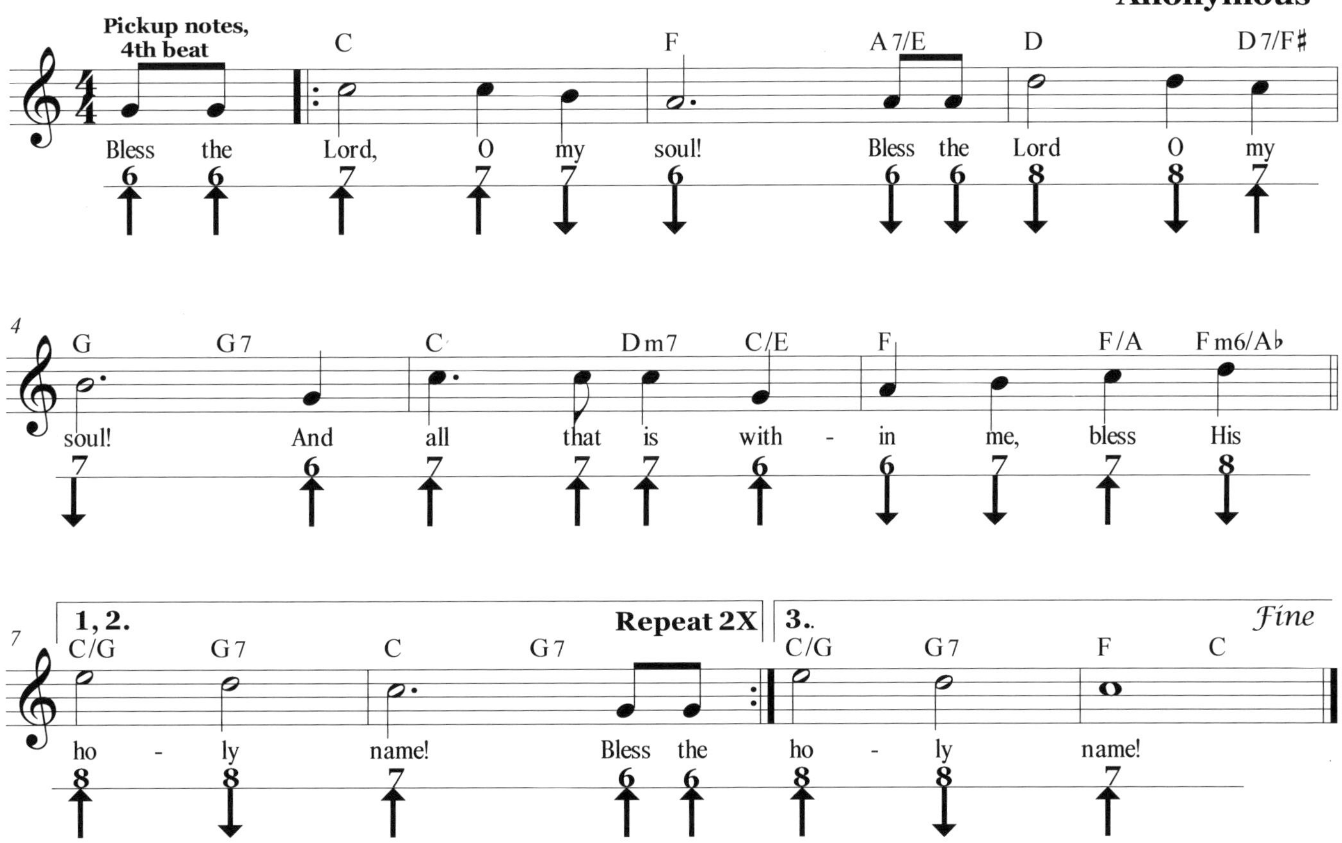

30

Sixteenth (16th) Notes *(two flags or two beams)*

Sixteenth notes are half of an eighth note. It takes two (2) 16th notes to equal one (1) 8th note. A note with two flags or beams. Counting:

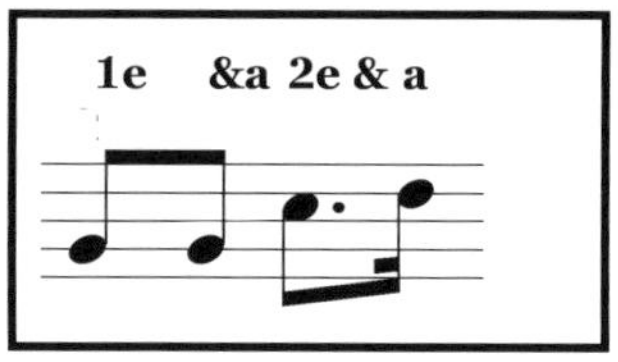

𝅘𝅥𝅯 = ¼ beat. A dotted eighth note: ♪. = ¾ of a beat. ♪. + 𝅘𝅥𝅯 = 1 beat

Blessed Be the Name (Chorus)

♩ = 105

American Melody

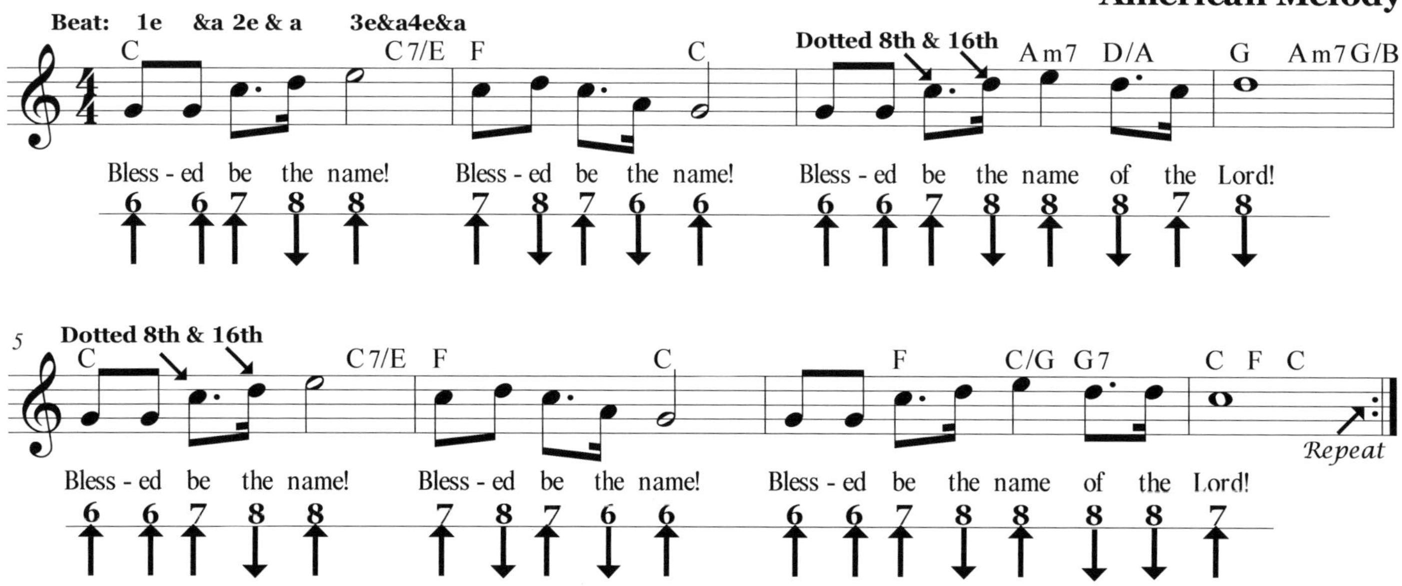

31

Precious Name

Lydia Baxter (1870) **William H. Doane (1871)**

♩ = 90

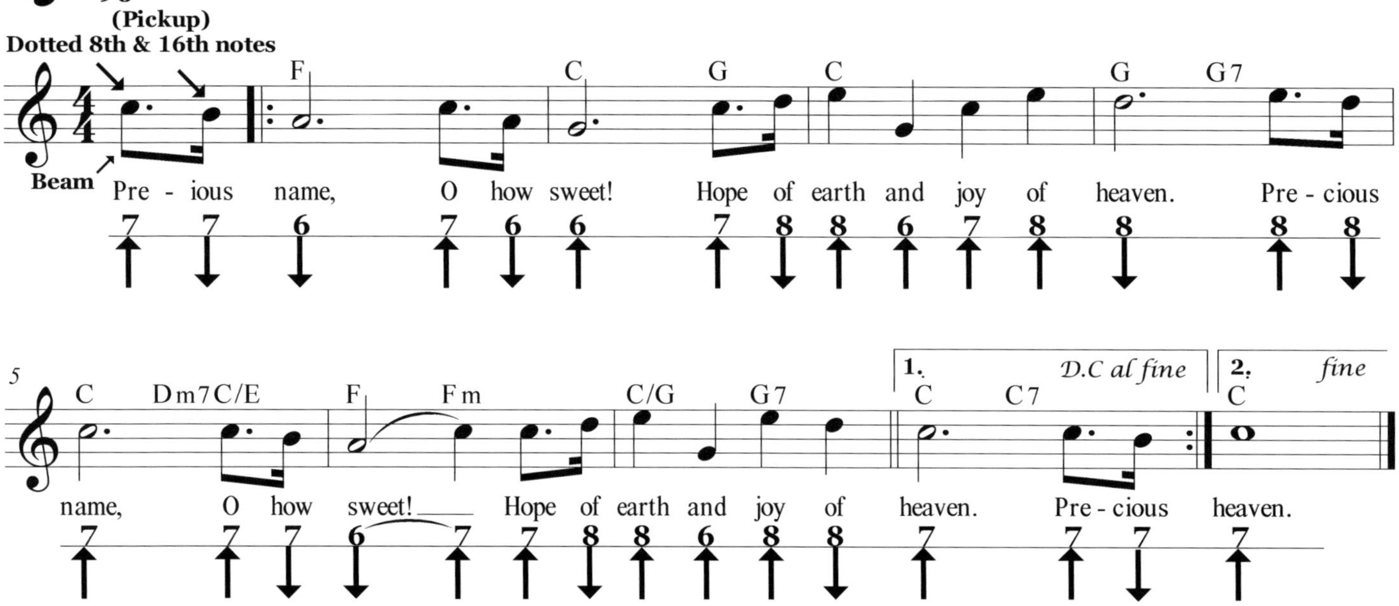

High f

f is on the 5th line of the staff. A **draw** note, 9th hole

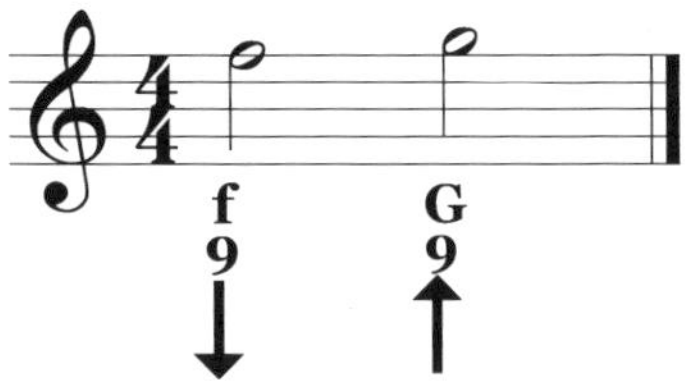

High G

G sits on top of the staff. A **Blow** note, 9th hole.

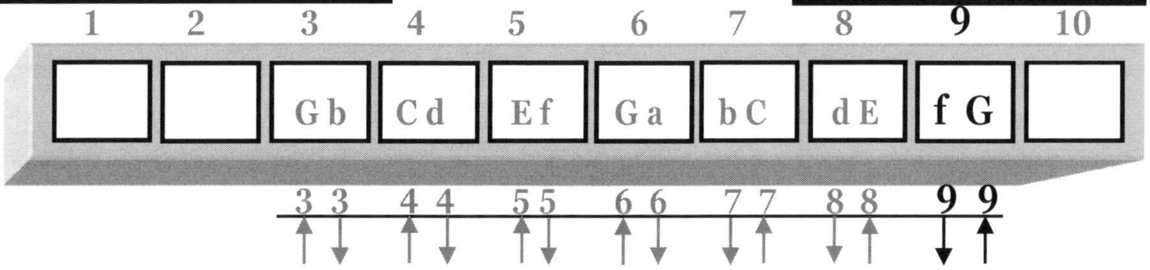

Only Trust Him

Words and Music by
John H Stockton (1874)

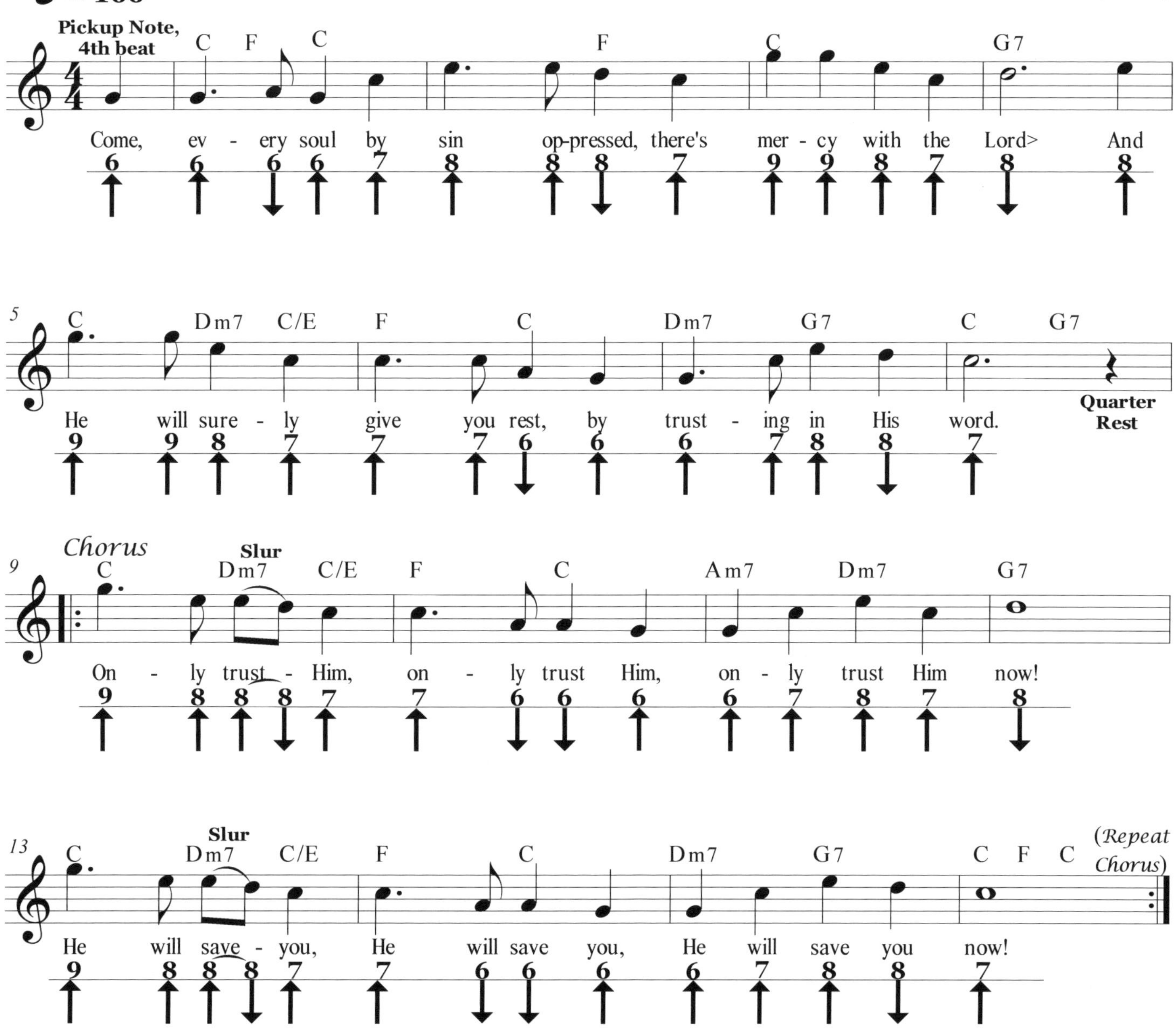

Key of C and key of A minor-neither has any sharps or flats.
'A' minor is said to be the relative minor of the key of C.

Reminder: From "the sign 𝄋" A direction of repetition from the sign. **Refer to page 28.**

O Come, O Come, Emmanuel

Latin Hymn (1710) **French, 15th Century**

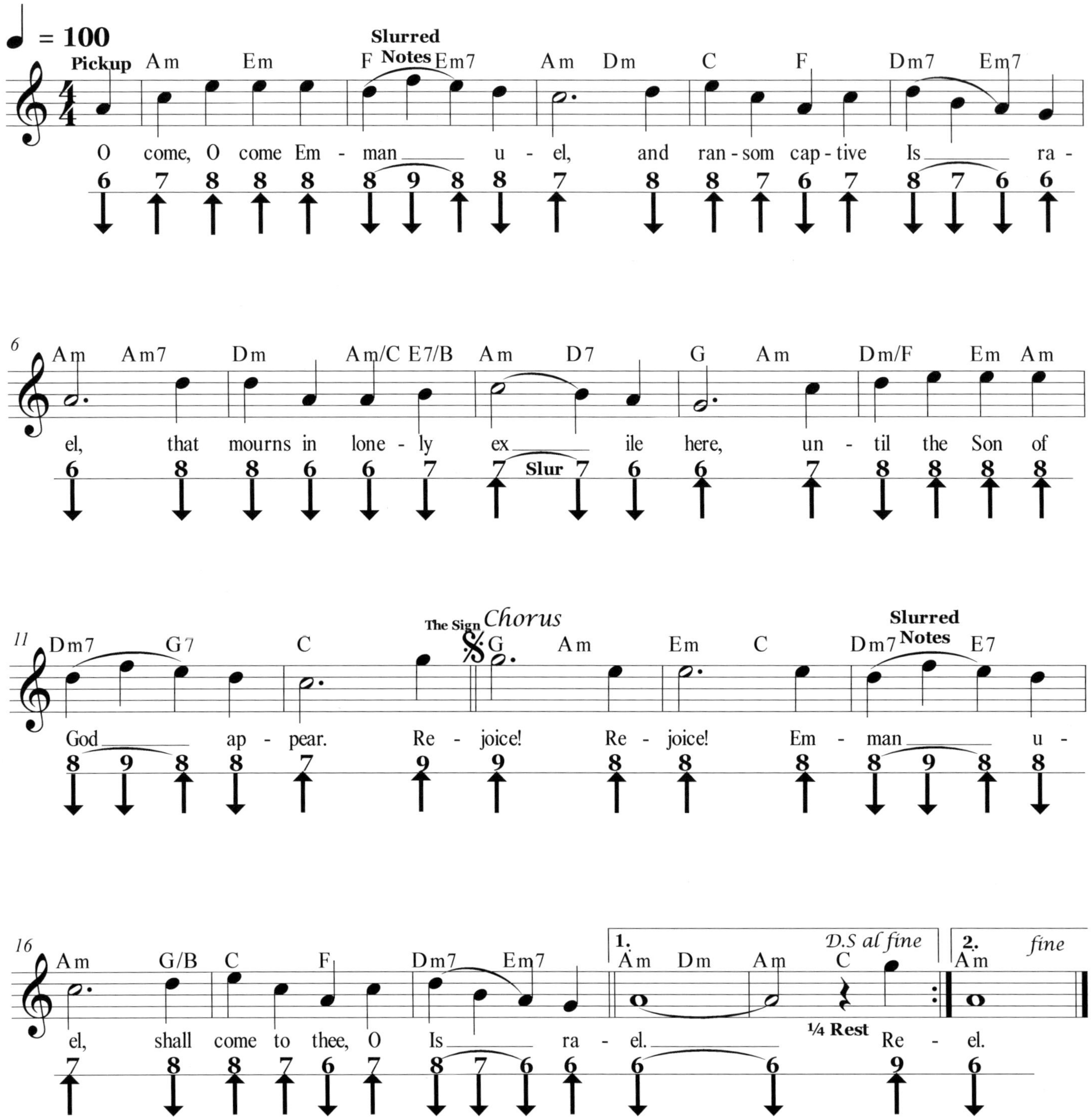

34

High a

High a is on the 1st leger line above the staff.
A **draw** note, hole 10.

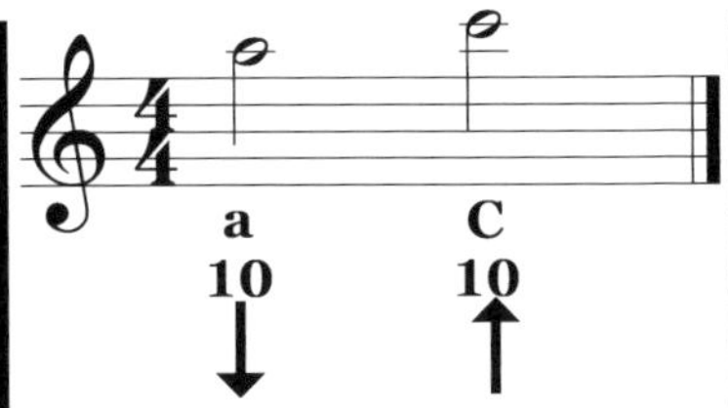

Double High C

Double high C is on the 2nd leger line above the staff.
A **Blow** note, hole 10.

There is no **"B"** note in hole 10.

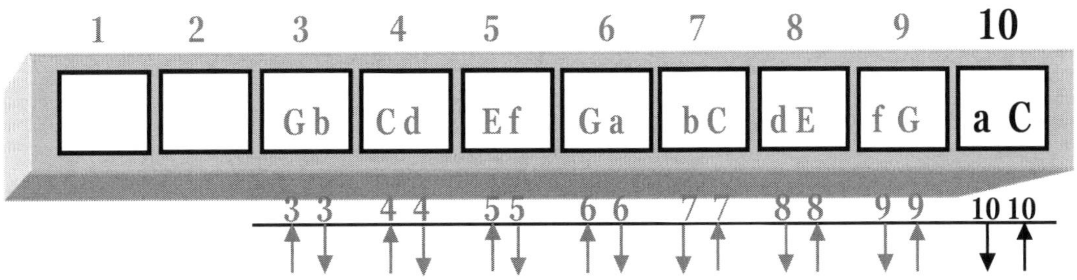

Begin, My Tongue, Some Heavenly Theme

Isaac Watts **Henry W. Greatorex (1851)**

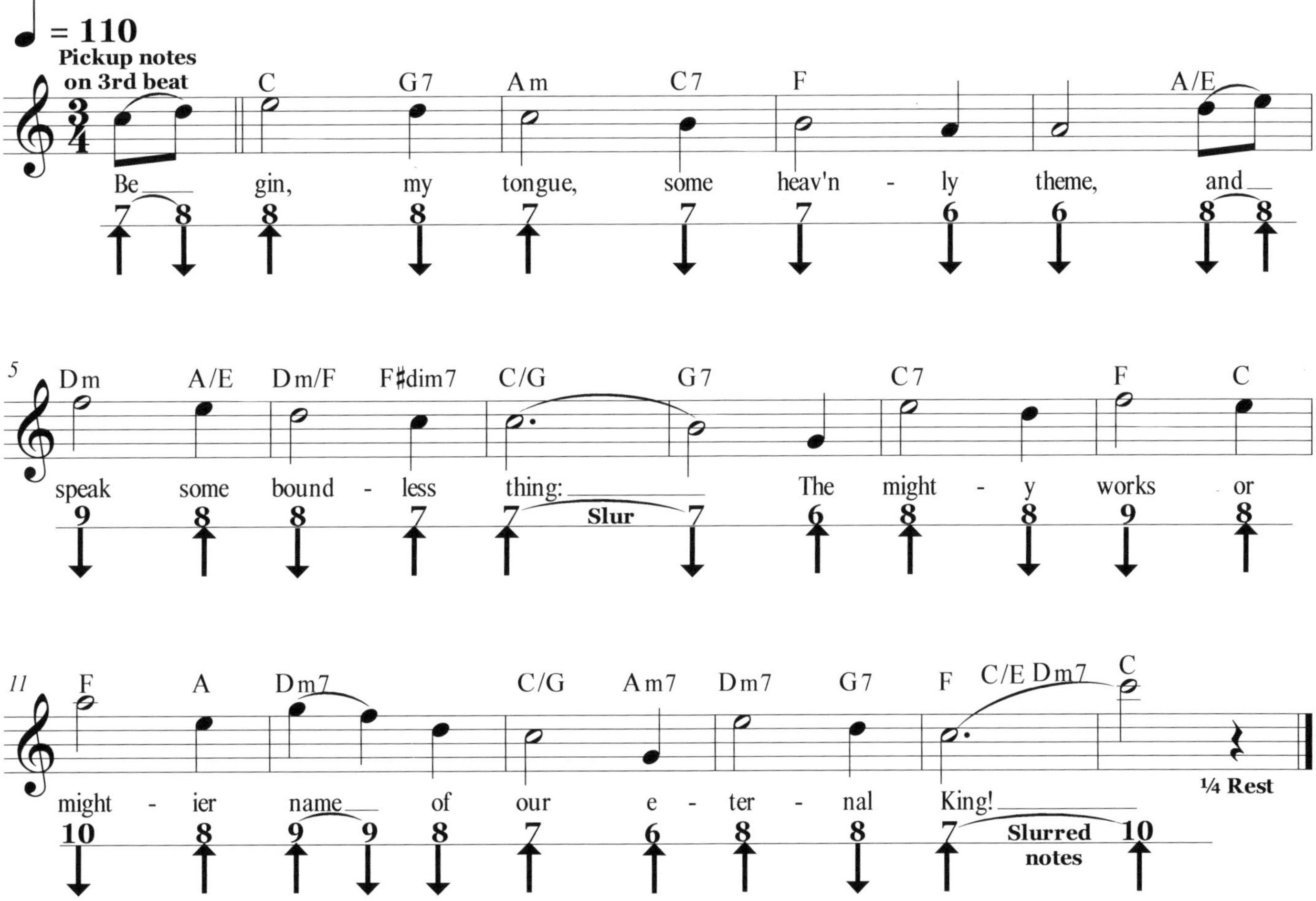

35

God Rest Ye Merry, Gentlemen

Key of "A" minor

Traditional **English Carol**

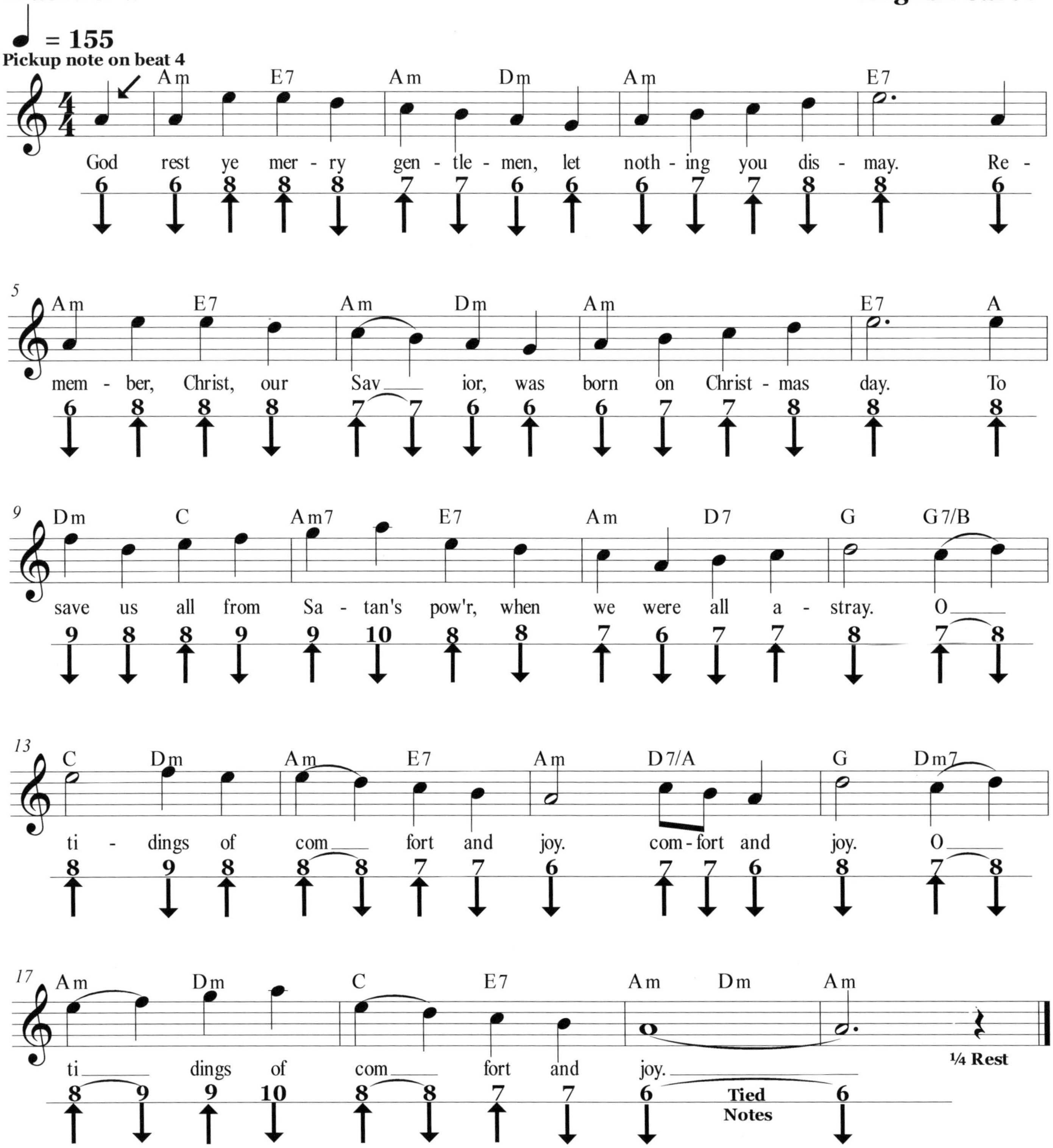

36

Reminders: 1st and 2nd endings-Return to the repeat sign, repeat then skip 1st ending, play the 2nd ending concluding at the word *fine*. Next, low 'b' is a draw note along with blow note low 'G' in hole 3 for solo playing below middle C. *He Is Lord* is another example playing the draw low 'b'.

He Is Lord

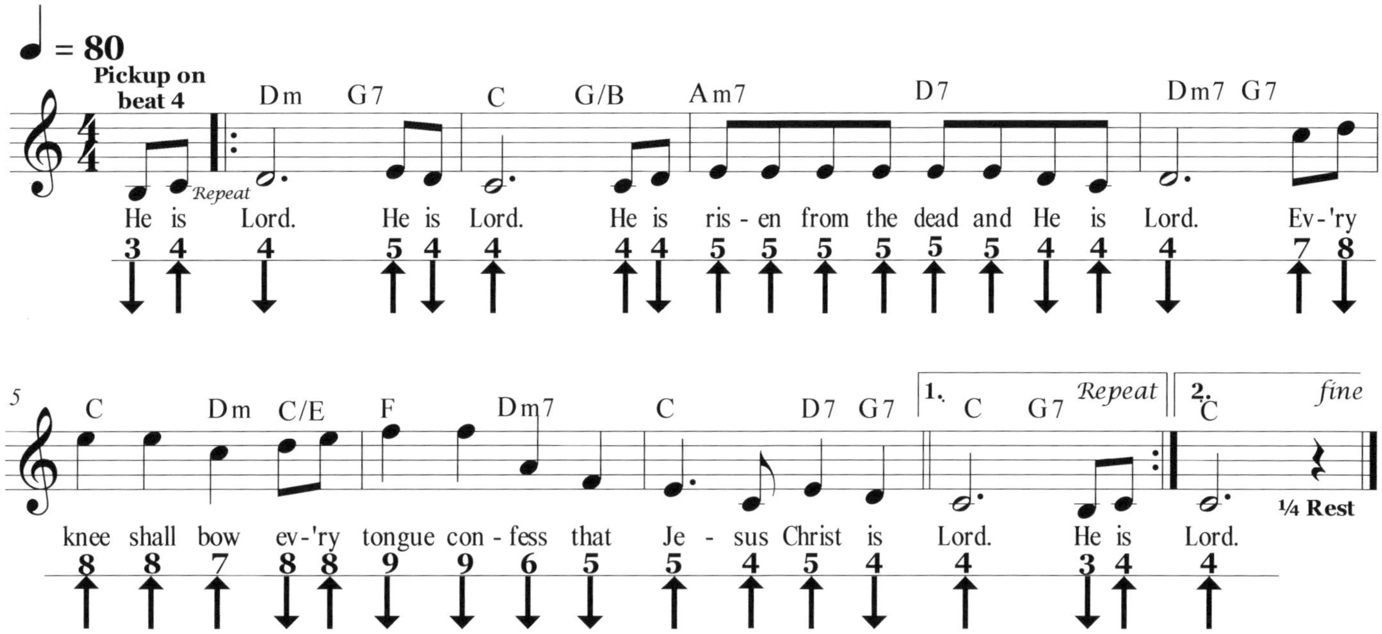

37

6/8 Time Signature: 6 = Beats in a measure
8 = Eighth note receives one beat

In 6/8, a quarter (¼) note equals **2 beats:** Dotted quarter note equals **3 beats:**

A dotted half note equals **6 beats:** Eighth (1/8) note equals **1 beat:**

Counting 6/8 Time (Emphasizing 1 and 4)

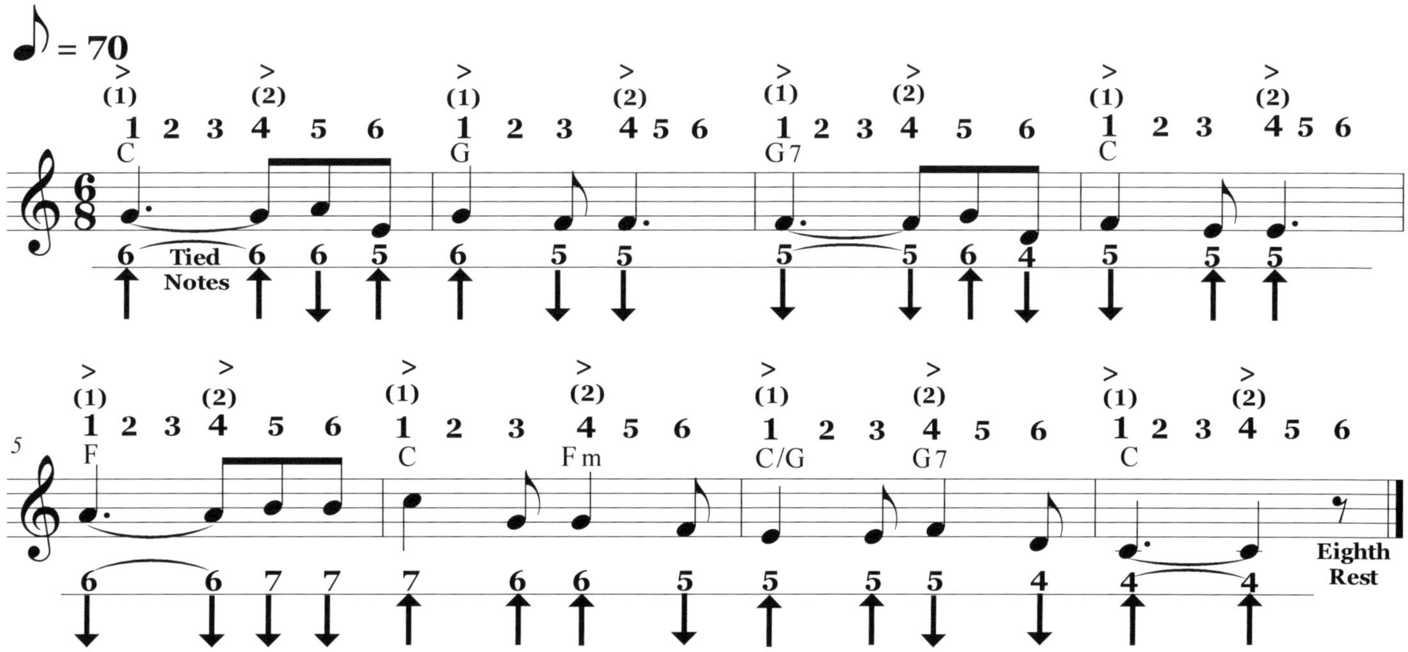

38

O How I Love Jesus

Frederick Whitfield (1855) **19th Century American Melody**

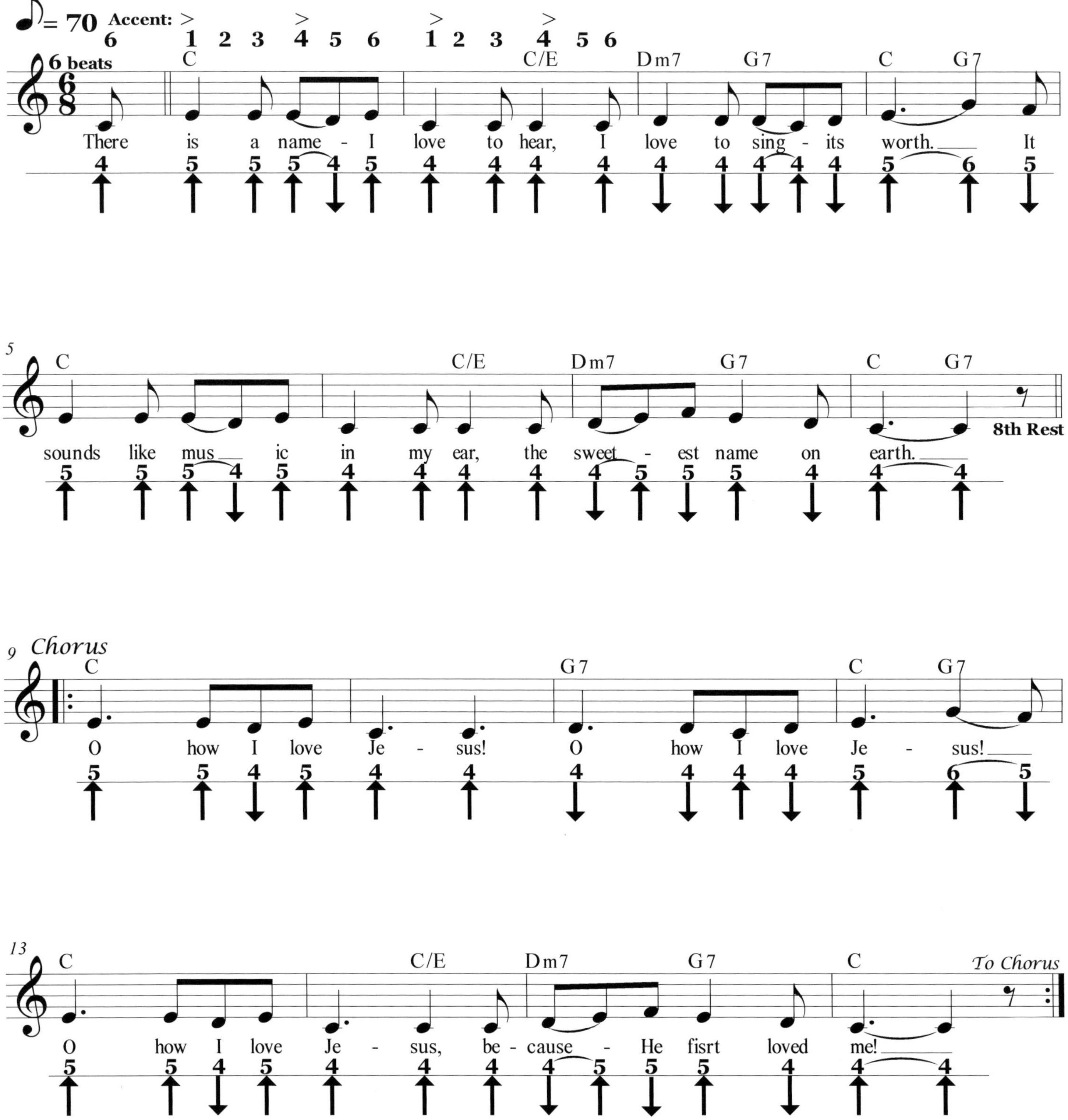

39

Open My Eyes, That I May See

♪ = 55

Clara H. Scott (1895)

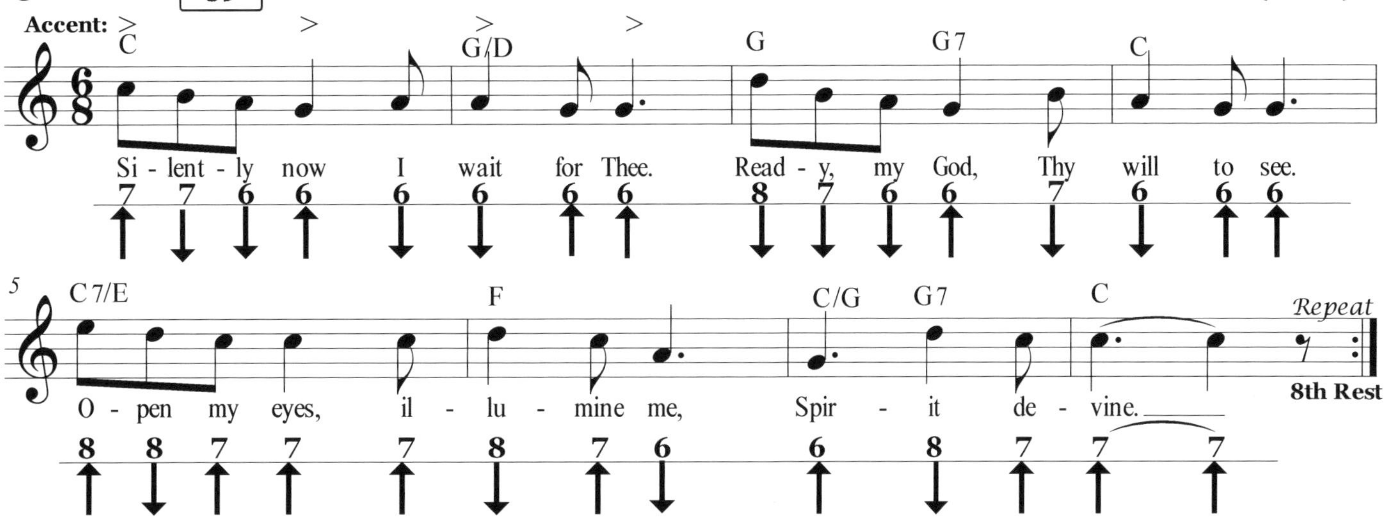

40

Jesus Is Calling (Chorus)

Fanny J. Crosby (1885)

George C. Stebbins (1935)

♪ = 60

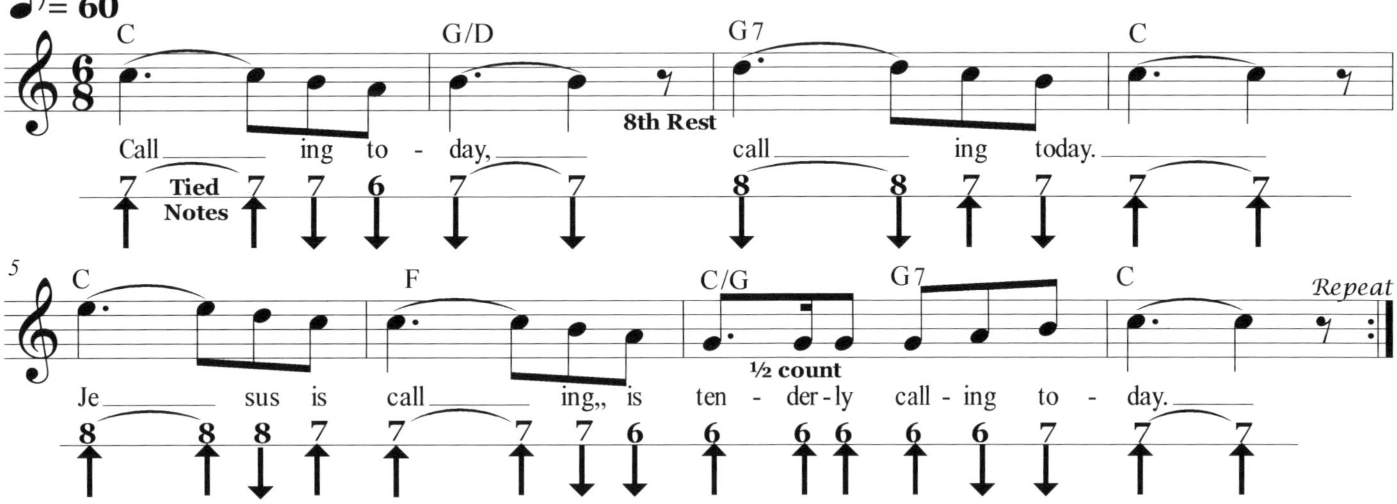

41

Lord, Lay Some Soul Upon My Heart (Chorus)

♪ = 55

Ira D. Sankey (1889)

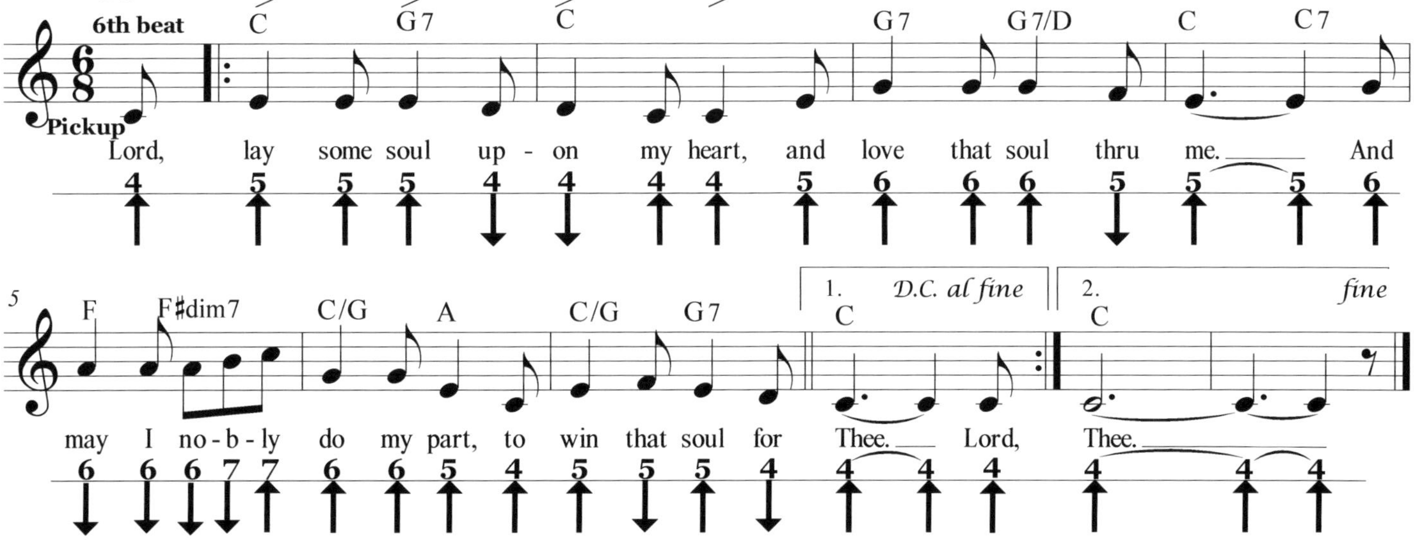

42

Reminder: *Repeat chorus* **(then skip *1st ending*, play *2nd ending* and conclude at** *fine***)**
Eighth note = 1 beat with emphasis on the 1st and 3rd beats

Love Lifted Me

James Rowe (1912) **Howard E. Smith (1912)**

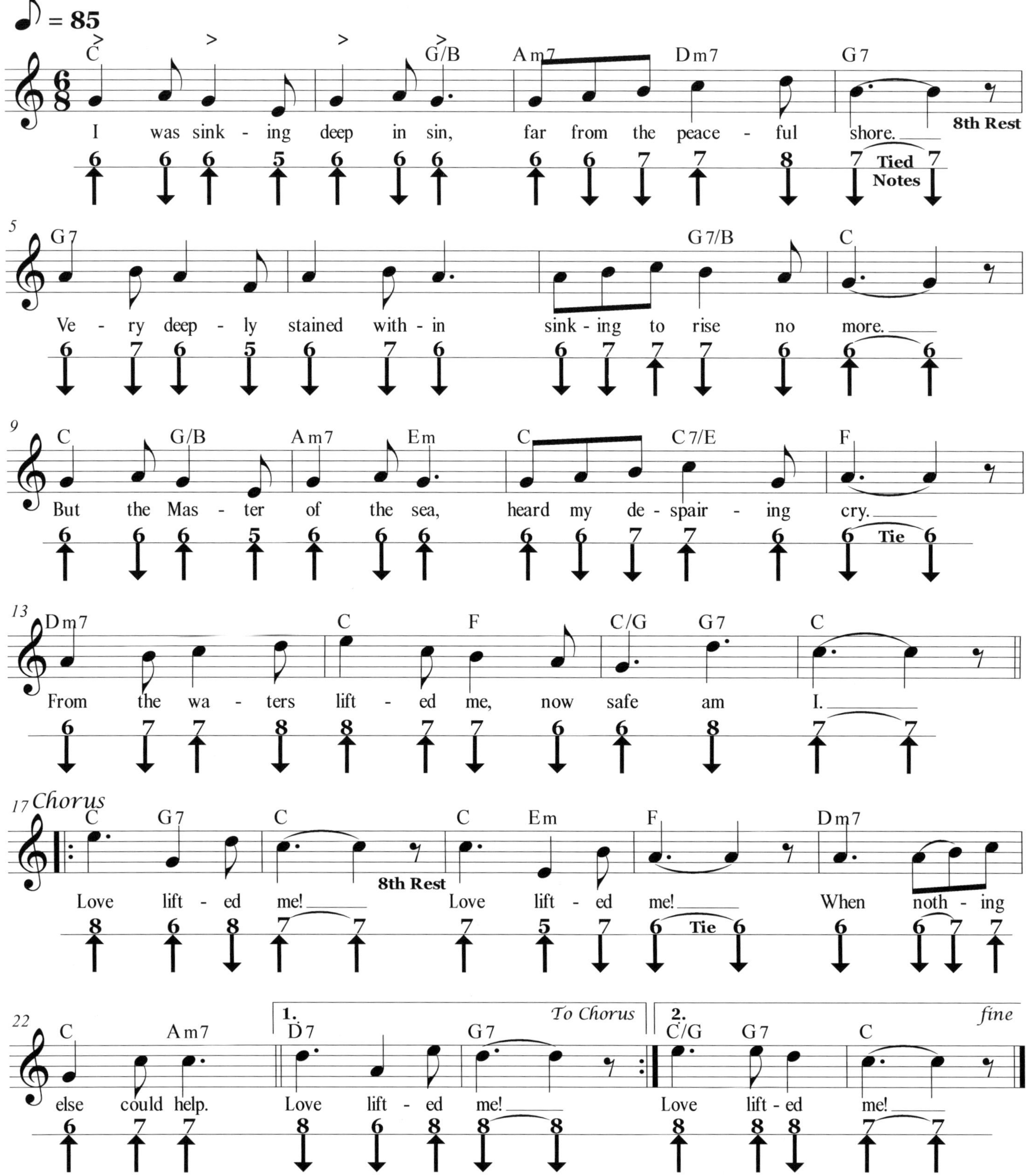

43

Low g draw

Low g lies below the 2nd leger line below the staff a **draw** note, **2nd** hole.

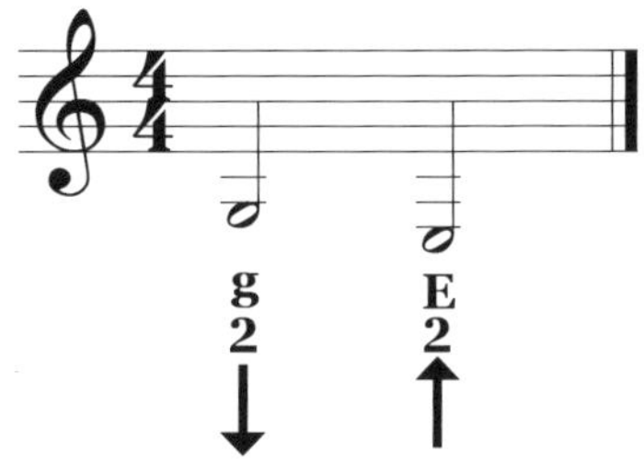

Low E Blow

Low E lies below the 3rd leger line below the staff, a **Blow** note, **2nd** hole.

There are two G's, 3 Blow and 2 draw. There is no "f" in hole 2.

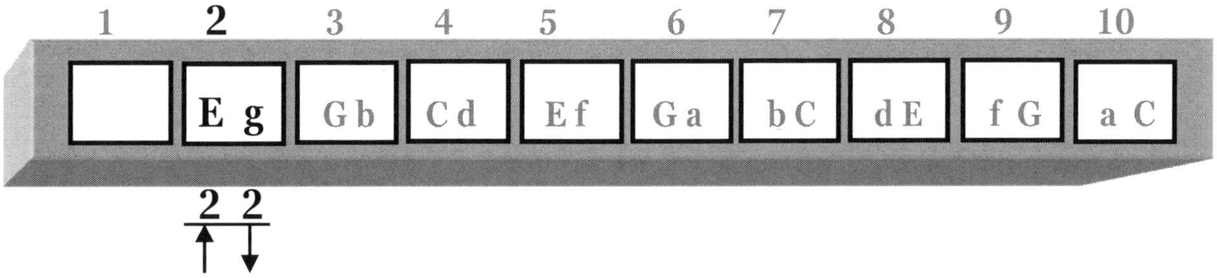

Low d draw

Low d is on the 4th leger line below the staff, a **draw** note, **1st** hole.

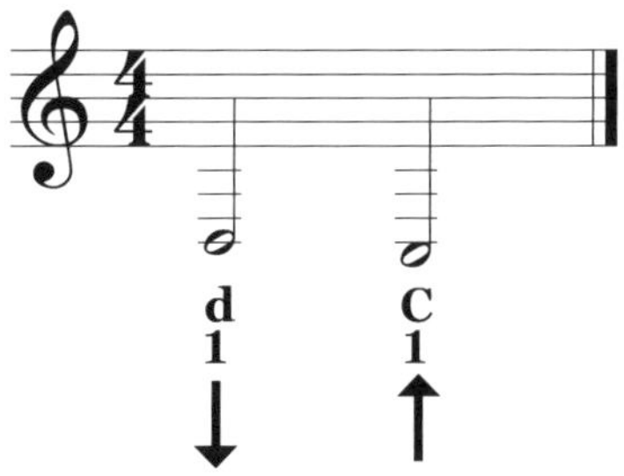

Low C Blow

Low C lies below the 4th leger line below staff, a **Blow** note, **1st** hole.

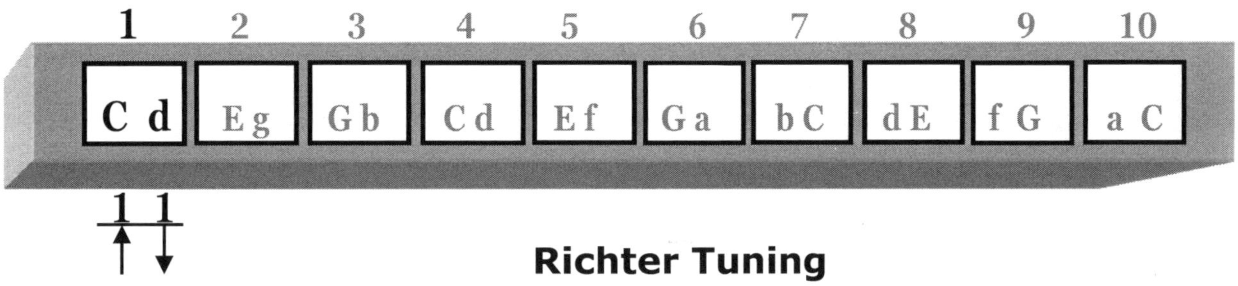

Richter Tuning

These lower notes on the harmonica are designed, with the missing notes of F and A, to play chords. This system is called the standard Richter-tuned harmonica.

44

PLAYING CHORDS

Holes 1, 2 and 3 along with holes 4 and 5 can be used for playing chords as mentioned on page 6. Playing three holes together forms a chord, blowing (exhaling) produces a C chord or drawing (inhaling) produces a G chord. The missing notes, 'F and 'A,' allow these chords to be played. See page 40.

1. Holes 1, 2 & 3 blow (exhale) together, produce a root C chord 'C E G'
2. Holes 1, 2 & 3 draw (inhale) together, produce a 2nd inversion G chord 'd g b'
3. Holes 2, 3 & 4 blow (exhale) together, produce a 1st inversion C chord: 'E G C'
4. Holes 2, 3 & 4 draw (inhale) together, produce a root G chord 'g b d'
5. Holes 3, 4, & 5 blow (exhale) together, produce a 2nd inversion C chord: 'G C E'
6. Holes 2, 3, 4, & 5 draw (exhale) together, produce a root G7 chord: 'g b d f'

Chords on Diatonic Harmonica and Staff

"Here, the music is written an octave *(8 notes)* higher than it actually sounds"

1. Root position C chord C E G: *Blow* 1, 2, 3 holes

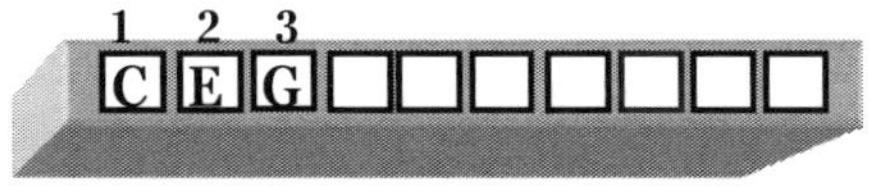

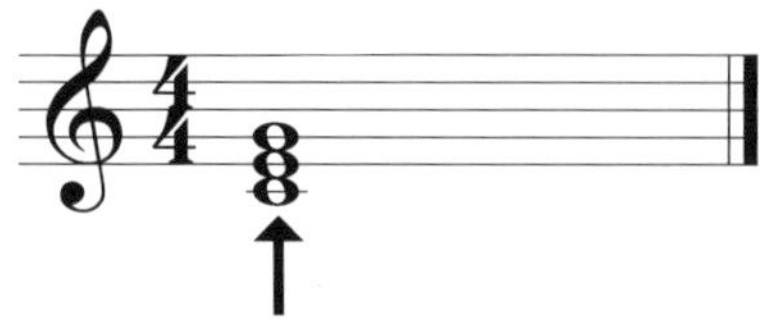

2. 2nd Inversion G Chord d g b: *draw* 1, 2, 3 holes

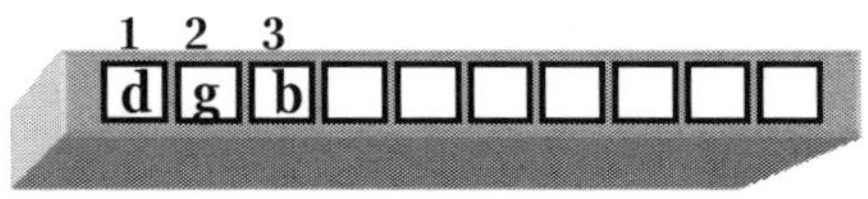

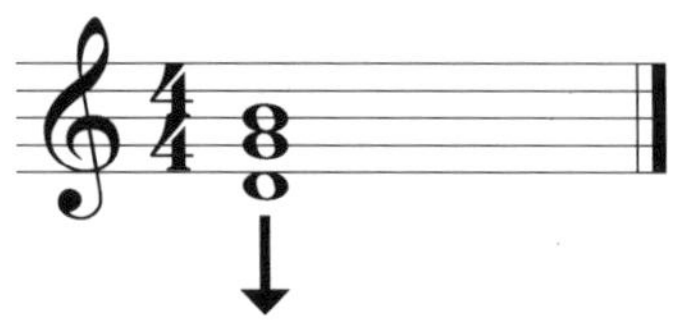

3. 1st Inversion C Chord E G C: *Blow* 2, 3, 4 holes

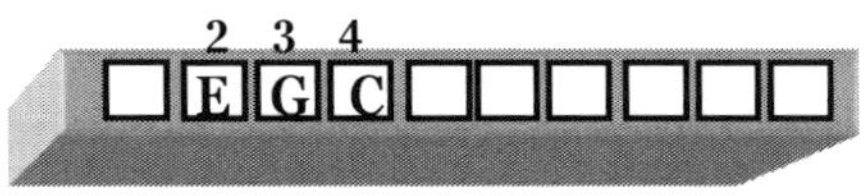

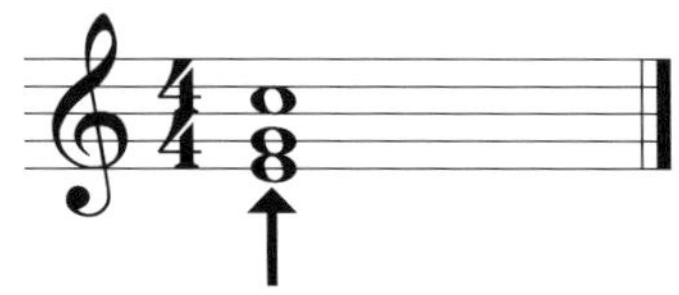

4. Root position G Chord g b d: *draw* 2, 3, 4 holes

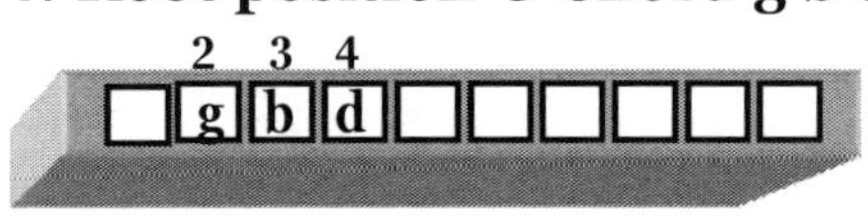

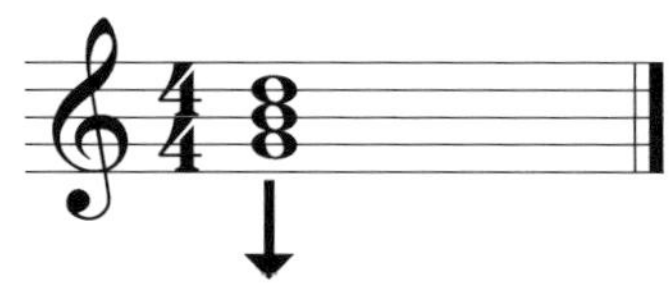

5. 2nd Inversion C Chord G C E: *Blow* 3, 4, 5 holes

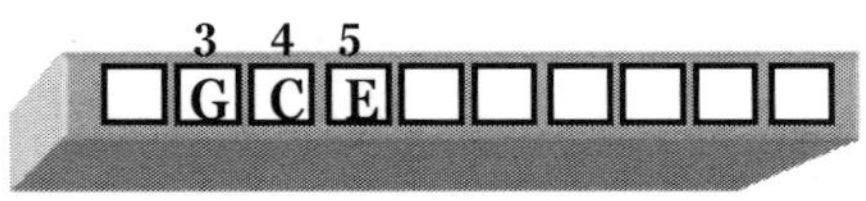

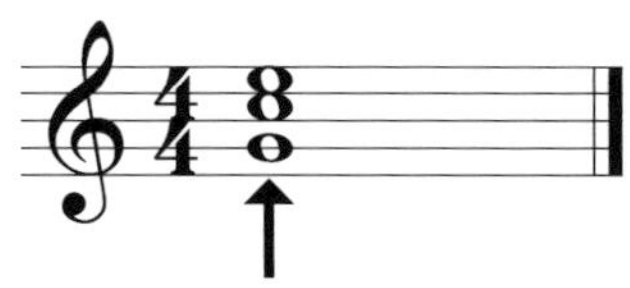

6. Root position G7 chord *g b d f* *draws* 2, 3, 4 & 5 holes

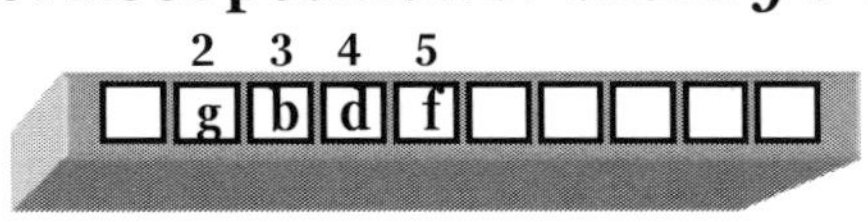

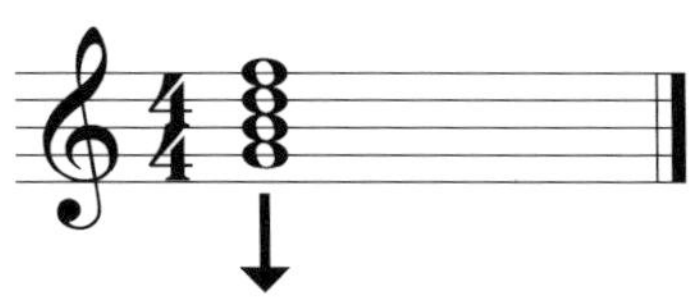

Play Chords for Effect

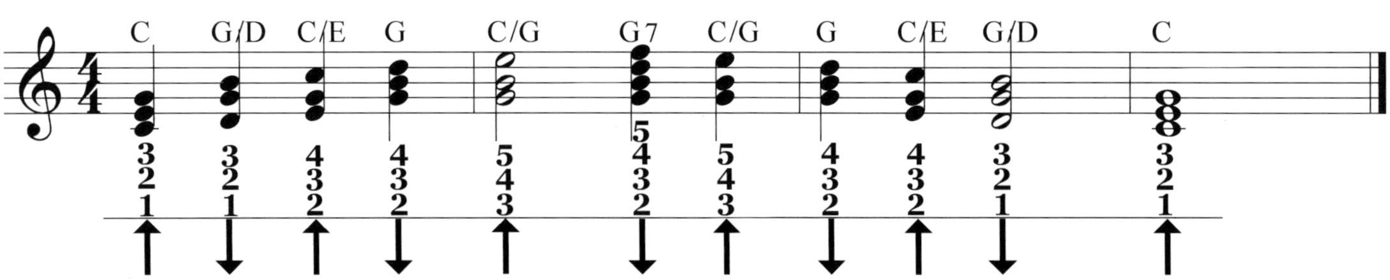